THE FICTION OF GLORIA NAYLOR

THE FICTION OF GLORIA NAYLOR:
Houses and Spaces of Resistance

MAXINE LAVON MONTGOMERY

THE UNIVERSITY OF TENNESSEE PRESS / KNOXVILLE

Chapter 3 was originally published as "Finding Peace in the Middle: Authority, Resistance, and the Legend of Sapphira Wade in Gloria Naylor's *Mama Day*". *College Language Association Journal* LII, 2 (Spring 1988): 153–69.

The appendix is taken from a personal interview, "Opening Up the Place Called Home: A Conversation With Gloria Naylor," Brooklyn, New York, May 3, 2007, and February 1, 2009. It is published by permission of Gloria Naylor.

The paper in this book meets the requirements of American National Standards Institute / National Information Standards Organization specification Z39.48-1992 (Permanence of Paper). It contains 30 percent post-consumer waste and is certified by the Forest Stewardship Council.

Library of Congress Cataloging-in-Publication Data
Montgomery, Maxine Lavon, 1959–
The fiction of Gloria Naylor: houses and spaces of resistance / Maxine Lavon Montgomery. — 1st ed.
p. cm.
Includes bibliographical references and index.
ISBN-13: 978-1-57233-722-0 (alk. paper)
ISBN-10: 1-57233-722-2 (alk. paper)
1. Naylor, Gloria—Criticism and interpretation.
2. African American women in literature.
3. African Americans in literature.
4. Home in literature.
5. Autonomy in literature.
6. Self-actualization (Psychology) in literature.
I. Title.

PS3564.A895Z77 2010
813'.54—dc22
2010015360

FOR

Mrs. Vina Jones,
Mrs. Lula Dockins, and
Mrs. Mollie Montgomery—
women who laid the foundation

Contents

1

Navigating a Blues Landscape:
The Women of Brewster Place

2

Burning Down the Master's House:
Linden Hills

3

Finding Peace in the Middle:
Mama Day

4

Mapping the New World Order:
Bailey's Café

Acknowledgments

My scholarly interest in Gloria Naylor's fiction began in earnest years ago when I was teaching a graduate course on contemporary black women writers. Since then, my fascination with her work has evolved with her publication of each subsequent novel. Rather than being an end of what has become a lengthy engagement with her work, this study represents a meditative pause in my ongoing critical investigation of Naylor's growing canon.

In a scholarly undertaking such as this, especially one that involves a vast amount of research, writing, and rewriting, there are individuals who labor in the background, out of sight and behind the scenes, in order to make that project a reality. I would therefore like to extend heartfelt thanks to Gloria Naylor, a consummate literary craftswoman and inspiriting influence whose writing continues to intrigue, challenge, and engage not only me but also countless other literary scholars. She has welcomed me into her home and made herself readily available in my attempts to gather insight into the intricacies of her life, politics, and artistic vision.

Ron Baxter Miller, Helen Burke, and Fred Standley offered invaluable criticism of the manuscript when it was in its nascent stages, and I am grateful for their wisdom, encouragement, and enthusiasm. I am also indebted to the graduate students who continue to share my passion for Naylor's works. On many occasions these young scholars caused me to rethink my interpretation of Naylor's writing, even as they challenged me to tease out the complexities of her multilayered canon. Joni Mayfield merits special mention because of her willingness to transcribe the interview in the appendix to this study.

Hunt Hawkins, my former department chairman, maintained a keen interest in the project and allowed me time to get the book done. My current chairman, Ralph Berry, was equally as accommodating during the completion of this project. As always, I am grateful to Florida State University for the financial support that provided the freedom from teaching responsibilities that enabled me to complete the drafting of the project.

Last but certainly not least, I would like to acknowledge my family for their love and patience, especially during the times when it seemed that this project was consuming nearly all of my energy and attention: my husband, Nathaniel Crawford, and my daughter, Samantha Natalya Crawford. You are my inspiration.

Introduction

Why did God make me an outcast and a stranger in mine
own house? The shades of the prison-house closed round
about us all: walls strait and stubborn to the whitest, but re-
lentlessly narrow, tall, and unscalable to the sons of night who
must plod darkly on in resignation, or beat unavailing palms
against the stone, or steadily, half hopelessly watch the streak
of blue above.
—W. E. B. Du Bois, *The Souls of Black Folk*

If I had to live in a racial house, it was important, at the
least, to rebuild it so that it was not a windowless prison into
which I was forced, a thick-walled, impenetrable container
from which no cry could be heard, but rather an open house,
grounded, yet generous in its supply of windows and doors.
Or, at the most, it became imperative for me to transform
the house completely.
—Toni Morrison, "Home"

The recesses of the domestic space become sites for history's
most intricate invasions. In that displacement, the borders
between home and world become confused; and, uncannily,
the private and public become part of each other, forcing
upon us a vision that is as divided as it is disorienting.
—Homi Bhabha, *The Location of Culture*

A predominant emphasis in the novels of Gloria Naylor is on the
ways that individuals counter the imposition of hegemonic authority. Opposition strategies figuring into her fictional cosmology may

entail group assertion, in the case of an urban community's attempt to challenge an intransigent political system hostile to the aspirations of the working-class poor, or they may take on a covert, individual configuration, involving a woman's effort to thwart a controlling slave master's unwanted sexual advances. Whatever form or scope these acts assume, they bear witness to the resourcefulness on the part of an oppressed people, the ability to utilize wit, guile, ingenuity, and other survival stratagems in order to hold at bay white supremacist rule.

African American vernacular forms, or symbolic acts of religion, speech, and music, offer the most telling and enduring evidence of black resistance in the New World. Whether they are rehearsed in the cotton fields, front porch, barbershop, storefront church, or ghetto streets, the stories and songs emanating out of the folk tradition not only encode the evolutionary journey from bondage to freedom, rural to urban setting, but also speak of the many adaptive strategies that have allowed African Americans to act independently of the larger society and survive whole (Smitherman, *Black Talk;* Smitherman, *Word*). It is therefore not surprising that Bernard Bell situates his identity as a cultural and literary critic squarely within the folk tradition, with its ironic "laughin' to keep from cryin'" sensibility. Bell describes his quest for scholarly authority, invoking the broad knowledge he gleans from both the academy and what he refers to as "down-home Jim Crow survival rituals and Northern school of hard knocks" (xv). This knowledge informs his interrogation of the rhetoric and poetics of the contemporary African American novel in ways that offer an enriching reading of a range of fictional works.

An investigation of houses and spaces of resistance in the fiction of Gloria Naylor, this study seeks to situate the myriad acts of insurgence in Naylor's first four novels within the larger frame of the places enabling black opposition to imposed authority. Of necessity, the work engages the residual oral forms revealing a confrontation with white rule. I argue that the preeminent site serving as a locus for the historic quest for freedom, autonomy, and selfhood is home, a nuanced, artificial construct bound with issues of nationhood and identity (C. Davies; hooks; JanMohamed; Morrison 1998). For Valerie Prince, the search for home serves as a basis for engaging representative texts in the African American novel tradition and she rightly attributes this quest to the displacement occasioned by the Great Migration, the move from South to North on the part of blacks at the beginning of the twentieth century (*Burnin' Down the House*). Using Hortense Spiller's essay, "Mama's Baby, Papa's Maybe: An American Grammar Book," which makes a case for the mother's primacy in black life and culture, Prince expounds upon Houston A. Baker's theory of the blues as a matrix for interrogating black cultural expressivity as she posits home as a space that is gendered female. The maternal is scripted into what Baker conceptualizes as a masculine site while Prince reaffirms the central role of women in everyday affairs. By conflating house and womb, her analysis highlights the gendered dimensions of the domestic arena in the black literate tradition.

Naylor acknowledges the close association between women and domesticity, as if in affirmation of Prince's theoretical assertions.[1] She also destabilizes the gender politics often linked with figurations of home when her male and female characters travel across the United States' landscape. Socially constructed conceptions of identity resulting in hierarchal distinctions between public and private, masculine and feminine, self and other are under constant interrogation in Naylor's growing oeuvre, which owes much of its impetus to the social dynamics emanating from her parents' working-class background in the rural South.[2] Equally as important in an appreciation of spaces of resistance, however, is her characters' flight along an increasingly global course that reifies not only the railway junction that Baker summons in his investigation of the blues but also the middle passage, the intermediate space between Africa and America figuring in postcolonial conversation as a site of transition and flux. For Paul Gilroy, the image of ships in motion is a unifying symbol for the transcultural movement defining a world-wide black experience (*The Black Atlantic*). The creolization that occurs as a result of cross-cultural exchange between nations renders set ideas of race and ethnicity obsolete. Homi Bhabha echoes this notion in architectural terms with his description of the stairwell as a liminal space between fixed polarities. The verticality that such a space implies, he contends, "opens up the possibility of a cultural hybridity that entertains difference without an assumed or imposed hierarchy" (4).

Naylor's penchant for imaginative, metaphysical settings and uniquely individual characters whose complex selves traverse predetermined cultural and geographic bounds points to a concern with the many transitional sites that mark not only an American site but also a specifically black, transnational historiography in ways that demand thorough critical investigation. Her authorial focus on communities in transit points to a unifying narrative within her canon. Such an emphasis also suggests a vital connection between her fiction and writing by African, Caribbean, and African American authors. The term "crossing over," which serves as an oblique reference to the multiple and often simultaneous passages in which Naylor's characters are engaged, conveys issues of migration, exile, and home figuring into the postcolonial narrative project. Within that conversation, the border subject is constantly in motion from one site to the next, and it is in what Abdul JanMohamed aptly describes as the interstitial space that the subject is granted the privilege of standing aloof from singularly constructed notions of self and forging multiple subjectivities that defy reductive attempts at categorization.[3] Bell hooks portrays this border region as a dynamic area of radical openness because of its implications for self-identity and agency (*Yearning*). One can form a potentially unlimited arrangement of selves, each one mutually constituted yet independent. Here, in the unmarked precincts between set cultural and national boundaries, the feminine replaces patriarchal models of self-definition as the maternal is restored to a position of power and preeminence. The implication of this reconfigured framework for border subjectivity is that the psychological fragmentation once coupled with a life lived within the larger society gives way to a fluid self—a multifarious, hybrid persona—existing at once both within and apart from the institutions of the majority culture.

A crisscrossing network of passages that invokes not only the migratory journeys undertaken by blacks in the continental United States but also the transatlantic voyage from Africa to the New World marks Naylor's fictional geography. As far as her novels are concerned, the middle passage serves as a richly evocative maternal site of becoming and possibility, a "matrixial border space," to borrow feminist film critic Bracha Ettinger's term, allowing seemingly endless options for identity, place, and narrative.[4] Because of the forced and voluntary travels defining the black experience, an ancestral home exists only in cultural memory and is inextricably linked with Africa or even the South, represented as ritual grounds for a reaffirmation of the expanded family relations and land-based economy sustaining African Americans before, during, and after slavery (B. Smith xix–lvi; hooks 41–49; Hurston 11–12; Davis, *Blues Legacies* 80). A key aspect of Naylor's authorial strategy involves the disruption of a seemingly seamless story or, more aptly, master narrative involving conventional conceptions of home, often figured in black writing as a contested space emerging out of colonialist ideology and praxis. As the daughter of southern migrants, she is an urbanite whose relationship with ancestral beginnings is as conflicted as the one Carol Boyce Davies attributes to Afro-Caribbean women writers in the United States. Davies asserts, "[The writer's] location in a variety of social and political contexts allows internal critiques of new inscriptions of coloniality and imperialism" (113). Naylor therefore troubles the fixed historiography underlying the North-South dichotomy, for instance, when she speaks of her grandmother's urban home as "southern"—despite its New York location. Recollections of her grandmother's Harlem apartment, a way station for a host of displaced southern relatives and friends, are vivid in their attention to detail. The residence was

> a weekend Mecca for my immediate family, along with count-
> less aunts, uncles, and cousins who brought assorted friends.
> It was a bustling and open house with assorted neighbors and
> tenants popping in and out to exchange bits of gossip, pick up
> an old quarrel or referee the ongoing checkers game in which
> my grandmother cheated shamelessly. They were all there to
> let down their hair and put up their feet after a week of labor in
> the factories, laundries and shipyards of New York. ("Hers" C2)

Reminiscences of the urban home as being "open" and "bustling" not only bring to mind images of the southern homestead with its open architectural arrangement and expanded domestic network but also challenge established ideas of a cold, sterile North peopled by a mass of indifferent city dwellers. The grandmother's residence, or, more precisely, Naylor's remembrance of this place, conveys an intermediacy that belies rigid notions of time, space, and identity. Later, in an expression of the continuing literary influence of that residence, Naylor incorporates the address of the apartment into the fabric of her debut work of fiction.[5]

The inscription of the domestic arena as a "safe space" and "site of resistance and liberation struggle" underscores the political di- mensions of place and its implications for identity formation in black women's writing (Hill-Collins 95–103; hooks 43). Toni Morrison's declaration that "matters of race and matters of home are priorities in [her] work" allows us to situate her fiction squarely within the discussion of resistance and home that has engaged Naylor's autho- rial attention ("Home" 4). For Morrison, the distinction between the metaphor of house and that of home is a crucial one in terms of the black woman writer's struggle for sovereignty as an author, an African American, and a woman. Her narrative project, like that of Naylor, is governed by the impulse to dismantle the master's house of race, gender, and class domination and fashion another space from which to employ issues relevant to America's racial politics. In this new space, a world situated within the perimeters of language, one informed by and at the same time existing apart from the dominant discourses of the larger society, there is liberty to move beyond the restrictive dichotomous existence W. E. B. Du Bois references in the first epigraph for this introduction and create a reality allowing the individual to reach a full, complex potential. Significantly, the space that Morrison invokes is not merely a rehearsal of the old paradigms delimiting female authorship. Rather, she speaks of a decidedly original domain—a discursive home—where not only a new subject but also new textual boundaries can emerge. The idyllic space that Morrison envisions is inextricably connected with the feminine and is analogous to Third Space or what Homi Bhabha describes as the in-between area located outside of predetermined cultural and geographic limits where the postcolonial subject attains an unbounded identity that refuses allegiance to singularly constructed notions of individuality (36–39). Here one is permitted to acknowledge and, ideally, embrace the multiple subjectivities necessary in the attainment of a hybrid self.

Naylor's first four novels constitute a tetralogy that mirrors her attempt to chronicle aspects of black history and foreground the epic search for peace, a veiled reference to a metaphysical place existing in cultural memory and encoded in the vernacular where parts torn as a result of the transatlantic journey are restored. In *Linden Hills,* a cautionary tale warning against the dangers associated with a life lived apart from the past and its sustaining traditions, Laurel Dumont's suicide is a direct consequence of her failure to access this place. The quest for peace culminates in *Mama Day* with George Andrews's ritualized journey to the chicken coop and continues on a multinational course in Naylor's fourth novel with the perilous voyage to Bailey's Café. Issues of liminality assume paramount importance throughout Naylor's canon with regard to the border subject's attempt to mediate the condition of being in exile and achieve a hybrid self that exists within and at times outside the institutions of the larger society. It is in the space that Victor Turner describes as a place of cultural limbo where the subject is allowed to achieve distance from an oppressive society and its destructive self-images and form a potentially unlimited set of identities.[6] My study argues that postcolonial figurations of the border region as a site of dynamic potentiality distinguish tropes of house and home in Naylor's canon from iterations of domestic space in texts by white female authors. While the concern with home may exist prominently in white female authored texts, the homes and subjects that appear in Naylor's first four novels owe no debt to artificially constructed notions of place or identity. Mae Gwendolyn Henderson is concerned with the ways in which the border subject's journey across boundaries into liminality—what she refers to as "border crossing with a difference"—functions as "an act of creation rather than one of violation" (26). Her pronouncements shed light on the tendency toward multiplicity or, to employ the term used to describe the uncharted region bounding the mystical Bailey's Café, "infinite possibility" associated with character and place, the two leitmotifs that unify Naylor's canon (*Bailey's Café* 76).

What is clear from a reading of Naylor's fiction is that her characters are ever in motion between regions, nations, and worlds as they attempt to find creative ways of acting independently of the larger culture in the construction of a safe haven, a uniquely maternal place of beginnings where one is allowed just to be. The following chapters offer an interrogation of representations of home as Naylor reinscribes a history involving black resistance and the adaptive strategies that have allowed African Americans to achieve an autonomous existence apart from white society and its killing definitions of the self. Narrative action in her first novel occurs in the era of the Black Revolution and Civil Rights Movement, with grass-roots efforts on the part of activists Kiswana Browne and Abshu Ben-Jamal in mobilizing a displaced community of southern migrants against the one man who owns the apartment complex at Brewster Place. Chapter 1, "Navigating a Blues Landscape," explores the viability of the community as a site enabling the largely female enclave to transform its bleak surroundings in the face of bureaucratic hostility and indifference. Naylor fictionalizes an urban community whose ability to draw upon the survival strategies emanating from an agrarian past allows residents to transcend the dire fate toward which the community seems destined. Brewster survives, and by interweaving vernacular forms from a southern heritage into the fabric of her debut work of fiction, she fashions a text representing a marked departure from the mid-twentieth-century urban realism novel and the pattern involving trenchant violence and despair.

Chapter 2 engages the dialectics of home and resistance through an investigation of the domestic arena as a locus for acts of subversion on the part of an unlikely subject: the upper-middle-class wife and mother. Marriage and family under bourgeoisie domination result in women's entrapment within a limiting role as Luther I, architect of the Nedeed dynasty, lays the foundation for the bondage subsequent generations of women experience when they marry only to discover that they are little more than their husbands' slaves. The Nedeed wives have much in common with their white female counterparts in the nineteenth century, but beyond that they share an affinity with a litany of black women—slave and free—who found creative ways of opposing the imposition of imperialist, aristocratic control. Among the Nedeed wives, housekeeping is laced with a revolutionary import that leads ultimately to an apocalyptic end of Luther's centuries-old masculinist empire. "Burning Down the Master's House" situates Willa Nedeed's life and death within a historic and political context involving insurgence on the part of the subaltern.

Chapter 3, "Finding Peace in the Middle," takes up the issue of Third Space and matters relevant to the construction of an intermediate site of autonomy and self-definition. As if in opposition to the household under patriarchal domination present in *Linden Hills*, Naylor seeks to fashion an alternative realm where women are allowed to realize their complete, multifaceted potential. Such a locale is patently female, with Sapphira Wade as creator and sovereign of the island paradise to which George and Cocoa return. Much like Sapphira's spirited rejection of the role ascribed to black women during and after slavery, islanders' resistance to commercial development is rooted in a past involving a vibrant folk heritage of independence and positive self-assertion. This chapter therefore seeks to locate such acts of aggression squarely within a framework involving tales of trickery, conjure, and black slave historiography.

Expanding the transnational emphasis of *Mama Day* with its account of the mysterious relationship between Norwegian-born Bascombe Wade and African matriarch Sapphira, *Bailey's Café* raises key issues of migration, exile, and home, but the text does so on a global plane. An eclectic group of postmodern citizens of the world crosses national bounds in search of sanctuary apart from the chaos and threat of widespread annihilation that world war presages. Naylor fashions a utopian domestic space that is male-friendly—one accessible to anyone regardless of gender for whom the search for home has proven elusive. As a place allowing individuals to redefine themselves in terms that encourage a critique of the politics of cultural representation present in the larger society, Eve's ambiguous boardinghouse/bordello functions as a maternal site where boundaries owing to difference cease. It is here that the novel's assortment of cultural orphans are to construct a unifying myth that will restore the sense of wholeness crucial to their individual and collective survival. The social order coming into existence in the novel's climactic scene with Naylor's conscious revision of the Virgin Birth is not merely a repeat of the old, predictable paradigms of house and home. Rather, Naylor fashions a household that is as much utopian as it is real, and it is one where imposed boundaries owing to race, ethnicity, and nationality no longer exist. Chapter 4, "Mapping the New World Order," examines the new, refigured textual boundaries heralded by the novel's magically real domestic space within the larger context of African Diaspora beginnings.

In Naylor's canon as in the tradition of black women's fiction, home is not exclusively architectural or geographic in nature.

Rather, it is a cultured, gendered space—one that closely resembles a highly symbolic signifying system bound with vexed issues of racial sovereignty and literary authority. On one level, home is simulated and associated with white, patriarchal rule, but Naylor's texts disclose the innumerable ways that individuals negotiate the restrictive places in which they find themselves, thereby wresting supremacy from those in positions of power. While domination is in the hands of those who fashion the public and private arenas defining a twentieth-century landscape, through a reinscription of the subversive, often clandestine acts of resistance on the part of the subaltern, Naylor recasts space in such a way as to undermine reader expectation and destabilize established models of dominance, influence, and control.

1

Navigating a Blues Landscape:
The Women of Brewster Place

Inner-City Blues

In *The Women of Brewster Place* Gloria Naylor situates the experiences of the folk within a sociopolitical frame involving the struggle for self-determination on the part of blacks in late-twentieth-century America. Organizational efforts by Abshu Ben-Jamal and Kiswana Browne recall the grass-roots activism of the Civil Rights and Black Revolution Movements as African Americans attempt to achieve dignity, equal rights, and freedom in a society polarized along race and class lines. What unites Brewster's residents is therefore not only an entrapment within the strictures of a hostile urban bureaucracy but also a dogged determination to defy the limitations of white, patriarchal control. It is largely a consequence of acts of insurgence on the part of the displaced masses that an otherwise dismal city landscape becomes a sanctuary holding out the possibility of fulfilled dreams.

Modeled after Naylor's grandmother's Harlem apartment building, Brewster Place is a recapitulation of a southern home with an extended family network, bustling activity, and creature comforts. The inner-city housing project is a way station attracting a diverse group of rural migrants whose arrival in the North brings into sharp focus the harsh living conditions in the crowded tenement, kitchenette, storefront, or boardinghouse. Not surprisingly, Naylor turns to Langston Hughes in the selection of "Harlem" as an epigraph for her debut work of fiction with a focus on the lives of those for whom the materialist American Dream is indefinitely deferred.

That Brewster is created as part of a clandestine arrangement between the alderman of the Sixth District and the managing director of Unico Realty Company underscores the oppressive political reality the community inherits. Formed in the immediate aftermath of World War II, the inner-city neighborhood has its genesis in the machinations of the rich and influential—power brokers who have a vested interest in maintaining authority over the masses. An amorphous power structure initiates Brewster's creation, just as it relegates residents to homelessness once Brewster is condemned. The revelation Abshu Ben-Jamal makes in *The Men of Brewster Place* that the community is razed in order to make room for middle-income housing lends emphasis to Naylor's continuing focus on governmental indifference to the plight of the working poor. Without the relative stability and safety that the neighborhood offers, Brewster's impoverished citizens are displaced and forced to take up residence elsewhere. Destruction of the brick wall, a reminder of imposed restraint, is a highly ambiguous albeit symbolic act paving the way for either a loss of solidarity on the part of the urban masses or freedom from the strictures of bureaucratic control.[1]

But Naylor is not so much concerned with the restrictions associated with life in the city as she is with the creative ways that the folk mount a challenge to authoritarian rule. Consider, for instance, the flight undertaken when fictional characters travel from one locale to the next, whether that trek involves the move from South to North or the passage away from Brewster in an attempt to find fulfillment in another locale. Following in the tradition of the blues persona who takes to the road amid tragedy and misfortune, Naylor's characters search and seek, engaging in the migratory journeys that encourage a critique of colonialist inscriptions of home. Residents of the failing community find that home is an elusive construct, and like the fictional neighborhood itself, it exists both everywhere and nowhere.[2] Much of the novel involves efforts to refigure Brewster's boundaries so that the neighborhood comes to represent the space associated with familial beginnings.

Mattie Michael's story, which chronicles her sojourn from Rock Vale, Tennessee, to the city, is instructive in understanding the role an urban landscape plays in Naylor's reinscription of places of origin. Brewster's central mother figure falls prey to the worldly, smooth-talking Butch Fuller when he entices her into a sexual encounter one spring afternoon. Understandably enraged as a result of his only daughter's pregnancy, Samuel Michael beats Mattie because she refuses to divulge the identity of her child's father. Margaret Early Whitt is accurate in her observation that Mattie's father is "an ambiguous character, stagnating in an Old Testament view of life" (20). He is every bit an authoritarian parent whose misguided attempts to control his only child result in her decision to strike out on her own. Samuel Michael makes enormous sacrifices for Mattie when he takes care of her while she is ill and hires himself out in the fields in order to buy her a pair of pumps. But the underlying point of Naylor's rendering of the father-daughter relationship is that Samuel Michael is largely responsible for imposing the puritanical standards contributing to Mattie's confinement within a gendered role. First in a long line of dictatorial father figures in Naylor's canon, he acts as an agent of patriarchal law by insisting that Mattie live up to his expectations regarding female sexuality. Her decision to leave her parents' once comforting, secure Rock Vale residence is as much an expression of her reaction to "the painful breach with her father" as it is a desire for independence from the stifling sexual mores of a provincial South.[3] Mattie's leave taking is voluntary, a consequence of the young woman's yearning to live life on her own terms, not those that her tyrannical father sets. Remaining in Rock Vale would have placed her in continued subjection to the South's rigid sexual politics, not to mention the ongoing tension between Mattie and her parents or the stigma associated with single motherhood.

Mattie shares a vital oneness with Brewster's colored daughters who find that their gendered identities cross the narrow boundaries that the larger society constructs, and she journeys away from her parents' residence, en route to the city, searching for a place where she can re-create the space she has come to associate with her rural beginnings, but on terms that would allow her to realize her potential as an African American woman. Although Mattie follows the course of countless others in her move north, Naylor's rendering of Mattie's journey, along with that undertaken by Etta Mae Johnson, highlights the role of sexual violence and domestic abuse in black women's decision to migrate (Griffin 44–45). In other words, Mattie's sojourn is a direct consequence of her subjectivity to patriarchal privilege and domination—a condition that continues despite her change in locale. Mattie is barely able to eke out a living wage. Uneducated and unskilled, she is forced to assume menial jobs with low pay and abysmal working conditions. Displacement is a recurring emphasis as she searches futilely in an attempt to find suitable living quarters. Out of desperation she takes up residence in an overcrowded boardinghouse that is a sanctuary to multiple residents. Here, she and her son Basil are forced to share a room while Mattie works as an assembly-line employee in a book bindery.

Much like the one-room tenement Bigger Thomas shares with his mother, younger sister, and brother in Richard Wright's *Native Son,* the boardinghouse underscores the lack of viable social and economic options for city residents. The squalid living conditions Mattie encounters become painfully clear when a rat bites Basil, forcing her to seek shelter elsewhere. Mattie is unwilling to compromise the safety and well-being of her only son, and her decision to move is born out of a determination to safeguard her family from the intrusion of the outside world. As is the case with her deliberate choice to leave Rock Vale, her departure from the cramped living quarters is as much an expression of agency as is the killing of the rat on the part of Bigger Thomas. Later, Mattie encounters the all-wise Eva Turner, who chides the young mother for leaving the boardinghouse: "Whyn't you just plug up the hole with some steel wool and stay there till you could get better?" (31) What Miss Eva fails to realize is that Mattie is by nature a survivor whose decision to move reflects her refusal to accommodate to her bleak surroundings.

As a prototypical account of the elusive quest for home among the urban dispossessed, Ann Petry's novel *The Street* sheds light on Mattie's dilemma. It begins with Lutie Johnson's frustrating search for an apartment, and the vivid description of the miscellaneous rooms she visits registers her dissatisfaction with her depressed Harlem environment. Singing offers an opportunity for the young mother to realize her dream of a better life, not only for herself but also for her young son Bub. By pursuing a career as a blues singer Lutie is to rise above the poverty that has characterized her existence. Petry is pessimistic about the ability of urban dwellers to transcend their harsh surroundings, however. Lutie remains vulnerable throughout her life, a victim of influences that are beyond her control. No matter how hard the young woman tries to reach her goal, the street prevails in its stranglehold over her destiny. Frustration because of a near rape prompts Lutie to resort to murder. The novel closes with a resounding note of hopelessness and despair as Lutie flees Harlem.

If there is a characteristic that distinguishes Mattie from her fictional precursor in Petry's work, it is the resourcefulness that Naylor's central mother figure exercises in coping with the demands of city life. Unlike Lutie, who is as much at the mercy of male desire as she is subject to socioeconomic influences, Mattie achieves a measure of dignity and autonomy within the perimeters of a largely female community. The ebony phoenix that the omniscient narrator references in "Dawn" serves as a trope for the black female storyteller who mediates between tragedy and despair, re-creating herself and her surroundings through a connection with a vibrant oral tradition. Lutie never has the luxury of finding refuge from the streets and patriarchal definitions of the female self. The boardinghouse she shares with Min, Mrs. Hedges, and Superintendent Jones reinforces her subaltern status in a world dominated by male predators and women who serve as agents of patriarchal control. Petry's benighted heroine is unsuccessful at reaching a place where she is allowed to exist whole. Mattie, on the other hand, redefines both herself and her inner-city environment through a link with a southern past.

While Lutie remains outside the bounds of the female networks sustaining Brewster's colored daughters, inhabiting spaces of "otherness" which her white employers and male sexual predators create, Naylor grants Mattie a chance encounter with Eva Turner—an elder wise woman who alters the course of Mattie's destiny. Naylor positions the elder woman at the liminal crossroads, a border region in religion and folklore that is rife with symbolic significance. Along the trajectory that Mattie follows, such a locale functions as an interstitial space that signals at once both the fixed polarities of self-identity available in Naylor's fictional world and the ability on the part of the black female subject to forge a self that is not bound by imposed limits. First in a continuum of timeless mother figures in Naylor's canon and the woman who guides Mattie toward the comforts associated with an agrarian home, Miss Eva is a rendering of Papa Legba, renowned African trickster god of crossroads and entrances (Whitt 23). Miss Eva's role involves directing Mattie and Basil away from the streets—a life of hopelessness, uncertainty, and displacement—and offering the single mother and son another chance at familial stability. Equally as important in an understanding of Miss Eva as a New World daughter of Legba is the timeless wisdom that the elder woman imparts. Naylor hints at Miss Eva's vast folk knowledge in the advice that the older woman offers Mattie concerning life, love, and relationships. Miss Eva has experienced multiple marriages and leads a fulfilled existence in spite of her singleness. Mattie may choose to dismiss Miss Eva's counsel as being the nonsensical meddling of an old woman, but the older woman embodies the fortitude and spirit that Mattie must embrace if she is to survive whole. Miss Eva's guidance, friendship, and intervention are to sustain Mattie in the face of displacement and loss.

The elder woman becomes not just Mattie's surrogate mother, but a sister-friend who provides the unconditional love and acceptance that Mattie forfeits with her move away from Rock Vale. A reconfiguration of the southern abode, with its warmth, conviviality, food, and conversation, Miss Eva's house is transformed into an intensely maternal space where Mattie finds the sense of belonging she needs. Naylor intends the reader to contrast Miss Eva with Mattie as the elder woman embodies the worldliness that Mattie lacks. Perhaps more important, because of Miss Eva's maternal presence, Mattie experiences a necessary shift in her evolving subjectivity—one that heralds the younger woman's metamorphosis into Brewster's central mother figure. Mattie becomes a child again as a result of Miss Eva's motherly influence. Consequently, Mattie, who is bereft of her Rock Vale family, regains the sense of cultural connection that she loses with her flight from Rock Vale. It is significant that Miss Eva refuses the rent payment Mattie offers. As if to distinguish the relationship between the two women from the landlord-tenant relationship subordinating Petry's Lutie Johnson to lecherous Superintendent Jones's objectifying male gaze, Miss Eva tells Mattie, "I ain't runnin' no boardinghouse, girl; this is my home" (35).

Although Miss Eva's spacious home is not the Rock Vale residence for which Mattie longs, it is a close urban equivalent. Mattie forgets about the painful leave taking prompting her move north and is consoled in spite of news concerning her father's death. Thus the eventual loss of Miss Eva's home is all the more heartrending. Without it, Mattie has no place to go. Like the beleaguered Breedlove family in Toni Morrison's *The Bluest Eye,* the novel inspiring Naylor to write her debut work of fiction, the single mother is put outdoors.[4] The eventual move to Brewster Place represents the failure of Mattie's dream of home ownership and belonging. Virginia Fowler is precise in her assertion that Miss Eva's residence is much more than just brick and mortar. It is "a symbol of nurturance and warmth and love and life, of Mattie's magical chance for another home" (30). Once Mattie moves to Brewster, her cherished plants, symbol for the rural environment that has nurtured her spirit, struggle for light on a crowded windowsill.

Mattie is far removed from the juke joints, cane fields, and shanties of Rock Vale. As if to counter the fact of her displacement, however, she successfully navigates both the emotional and geographic topography of her depressing urban locale, becoming Brewster's quintessential mother who remakes herself and her reality through an association with the agrarian setting from which she hails. Alone and impoverished, Mattie has few viable options left. Basil has abandoned her and she has little to speak of in the way of marketable job skills. But here again *The Bluest Eye* is instructive. Like the prostitutes China, Marie, and Poland, who live one story above the troubled Breedlove family, removed from the tragic fate that engulfs Pecola, Mattie not only transcends the turmoil existing just beyond Brewster's dead end street but also, through her example of black female resilience, paves the way for a redefinition of the traditional roles and spaces to which African American women are consigned.

Naylor's deliberate use of architectural space serves as a commentary on the ways in which African Americans in general and black women in particular fashion safe spaces that hold at bay white supremacist rule.[5] Outside the perimeters of Brewster Place, Naylor's fictional characters are subject to white society and its limiting definitions of blackness. Within the black community, however, in places such as the home, church, community center, barbershop, or beauty parlor, African Americans are allowed to forge bonds that negate the destructive effects of white authority. Patricia Hill Collins makes an important distinction between the institutional sites proscribed by the larger society and those within the black community allowing women to develop positive self-images. Collins asserts, "Extended families, churches, and African-American community organizations are important locations where safe discourse potentially can occur" (95). She goes on to suggest that "[i]nstitutions controlled by the dominant group such as schools, the media, literature, and popular culture are the initial source of externally defined, controlling images. African-American women have traditionally used Black families and community institutions as places where they could develop a Black woman's culture of resistance" (95).

Naylor's placement of Mattie in an upstairs apartment is an affirmation of the woman's ability to create a psychological buffer from the painful realities of inner-city life. Similarly, neighborhood activist Kiswana Browne, in voluntary exile from her parents' upper-middle-class neighborhood, lives upstairs with a vantage point that permits a glimpse of the social and economic possibilities beyond Brewster's boundaries. It is because of this vision that Kiswana works tirelessly in order to mobilize the otherwise fragmented community against the one man who owns the decaying building.

A consideration of the spatial politics involved in Brewster's configuration paves the way for a reading of the novel that is more positive than the one Michael Awkward offers.[6] This is not to say, however, that Naylor is not on one level ambivalent about the viability of the spaces of resistance within the black community. Etta Mae Johnson succumbs to the seductive powers of Reverend Moreland Woods at Canaan Baptist Church, an institution that mirrors the exploitative practices and crass materialism of the larger society. Brewster's insistent homophobia takes its toll on lesbians Theresa and Lorraine, who find that the neighborhood is anything but a safe haven for individuals whose sexuality traverses heterosexual bounds. Lorraine is relegated to the forbidden margins of the community, alone in a darkened, secluded alley following C. C. Baker's vicious rape. Ben, who is unable to come to grips with his past, resides in a basement apartment, outside Brewster's revitalizing female bonds in a space reserved for the subaltern.

But the persistence of female bonds, girl talk, and especially the blues not only offers evidence of the buoyancy on the part of the urban folk, these adaptive strategies reveal the black subject's ability to navigate away from the role of passive victim. Consider the place of the blues in ritualizing the metamorphosis that Etta undergoes during her move to Brewster Place. That Naylor intends for the reader to draw comparisons between Etta and a community of black female blues singers is evident from the use of lyrics by Billie Holiday throughout Etta's narrative. The specter of Holiday hovers over Etta's story with lines from classic tunes serving as an intertext that echoes and foreshadows events in Etta's tumultuous life. Brewster's wandering resident is rebellious, at least according to the mores of southern society, by virtue of her refusal to embrace a traditional identity: "Rock Vale had no place for a black woman who was not only unwilling to play by the rules, but whose spirit challenged the very right of the game to exist" (59). Etta is her own woman and refuses to acquiesce to anyone else's standards.

Nowhere is Etta's nonconformity more evident than in her relations with men. Her narrative suggests male-female relations as a site for critiquing socially prescribed notions of woman's place. It is out of a spirit of independence that she rejects unwanted advances on the part of Johnny Brick, the "horny white bastard" who sees her as a sexual conquest (60). As far as he is concerned, she is little more than sexual plaything whose sole purpose is to gratify his lust. Although Naylor does not divulge exactly what transpires between Etta and Brick, it is safe to assume that the fiercely defiant woman inflicts a great deal of emotional or physical harm—so much damage that his relatives retaliate by pursuing her and later burning down her father's barn. Etta could have surrendered to Brick's sexual advance. Instead, she chooses to maintain her autonomy through an act of aggression directed toward white patriarchy as much as against Brick himself.

Simeon fares no better in his relationship with the feisty woman who steals both his car and underwear before fleeing Rock Vale. Fear of his wife's reprisal prompts him to remain silent about the incident rather than report it to the authorities. Otherwise, Etta would have found herself in direct confrontation with the law. Aside from the rather humorous accounts of Etta's hair-scraping adventures, it is the resounding laughter permeating Mattie's living room as Etta recounts her exploits that is telling in an understanding of the blues landscape that Brewster's colored daughters navigate. That laughter, no less than the tears the women shed, serves in a cathartic sense as what Jenny Brantley describes as a source of salvation for Naylor's female characters.[7] The laughter the women share also harks back to the novel's oral roots in the folk tradition and a survivalist ethnic involving black triumph over adversity. Because of the women's ability to achieve a psychological distance from an oppressive reality, Mattie's sparsely furnished living room becomes a free space, an intermediate site of becoming reminiscent of the urban North figuring in the slave narrative. Both Etta and Mattie escape the either-or binary that would entrap the black female subject in the role of passive, subservient victim. The two women achieve a profound sense of liberty in the safe harbor of each other's company. In ways that signal the formation of a specifically feminine space existing outside the boundaries of white patriarchy, the omniscient narrator describes the women's circuitous journey to Brewster Place as a female rite of passage: "Etta and Mattie had taken totally different roads that with all of their deceptive winding had both ended up on Brewster Place. Their laughter now drew them into a conspiratorial circle against all the Simeons outside of that dead-end street, and it didn't stop until they were both weak from the tears that flowed down their faces" (61).

Etta is understandably devastated after her embarrassing one-night stand with Moreland Woods, one of many debauched preachers in Naylor's canon. Her hopes for marriage and upward socioeconomic mobility are dashed with her ignominious return to the failing community. When the bold, brassy woman goes back to Brewster, she reaches the depths of her troubled life and sees the neighborhood in starkly realistic terms: "Now it crouched there in the thin predawn light, like a pulsating mouth awaiting her arrival. She shook her head sharply to rid herself of the illusion, but an uncanny fear gripped her, and her legs felt like lead. If I walk into this street, she thought, I'll never come back. I'll never get out. Oh, dear God, I am so tired—so very tired" (73). Etta's return to the dilapidated housing project is figured in terms richly evocative of a descent into an abyss. Once back there, the aging Etta Mae Johnson bears little resemblance to the lively, outspoken woman that residents came to know. As a result of her willingness to embrace the transformational message of the blues, however, Etta liberates herself from the strictures of passivity and victimization, thereby transforming an otherwise painful situation into a place where self-definition can occur. The stairway leading to Mattie's residence signals the presence of an interstitial space between fixed polarities where Etta is able to forge a fluid identity existing apart from a white male society and its valuations. Etta thus exchanges her status as victim for that of survivor. Brewster Place, with all of its poverty, loss, and disappointment, loses its insistent stranglehold on her while the margins, once figured as a space of enclosure, limitation, and finality, become a dynamic site of transformation.

Mattie is the reliable sister-friend who stays up in anticipation of Etta's inevitable return. The illuminated lamp in Mattie's living room is what Gaston Bachelard describes as a "symbol of perpetual waiting" (46). Yet the room assumes such positive associations because of the persistent bond uniting the two southern sisters—a bond solidified by the blues lyrics wafting from Mattie's living room. The apartment becomes a welcoming, maternal setting, not of itself but as a result of the women's emotional response to life's inevitable contradictions. Like a single yet triumphant Janie at the close of Zora Neale Hurston's *Their Eyes Were Watching God,* Etta thus ascends toward "the light and the love and the comfort that awaited her" (74). The restless woman will likely leave again because it is her nature to wander and search. At her story's end, however, she is at peace, anchored amid a community of indomitable women.

Of Housewives and Revolutionaries

Naylor presents a portrait of an urban community poised on the brink of sociopolitical change, and in her rendering of Brewster's evolutionary move into the late twentieth century, she foregrounds the acts of insurgence on the part of the slumbering masses—the nameless, faceless denizens of the city—who possess the latent potential to alter themselves and their everyday reality. At the forefront of Brewster's political awakening are the women who play an important, albeit unacknowledged, role in bringing about the radically transformed future heralded by the block party, Mattie's dream of a unified community engaged in a struggle for freedom and self-determination. It is in the account of the women's communal efforts to tear down the brick wall that the reader glimpses Naylor's gendered reinscription of the story involving the black quest for independence. Kiswana Browne's commitment to grass-roots activism prompts her to align herself with the poor and the daily challenges they face. Although her organizational efforts are frustrated at every turn, she joins the group of women assembled in the novel's climactic story as they dismantle the imposing brick wall. Kiswana may find that her dream of a unified, empowered community is at least temporarily deferred, but it is the persistence of her dream of a better future that both solidifies her bond with Brewster's colored daughters and prompts her to persevere.

"The Block Party," the culminating narrative and most problematic of the seven stories that comprise Naylor's debut work of fiction, is indeed what Jill Matus refers to as "everyone's story."[8] Each woman therefore dreams of Lorraine so as to convey the oneness between Brewster's colored daughters that belies notions of sexual difference. Even though residents attempt to exclude the lesbian couple from the nurturing bond of friendship uniting the women as one collective body, Theresa and Lorraine's frustrating efforts at inclusion suggest that the lesbian couple has more in common with Brewster's colored daughters than the community realizes.

That the novel climaxes with a utopian portrait of a group effort to tear down the brick wall points to a revolutionary emphasis grounded in the twentieth-century American fight for self-determination. Such an effort on the part of Naylor's fictional characters is cultured and gendered, with black women figuring as powerful agents of sociopolitical change. In this regard, the novel directs attention to not only the role of everyday individuals in the quest for freedom but also the place of mothers and motherhood as instruments of empowerment and community uplift. Naylor's female characters have much in common with historical figures such as

Fannie Lou Hamer and Mary McLeod Bethune, activist women at the forefront of the modern Civil Rights Movement. Paula Giddens's *When and Where I Enter: The Impact of Black Women on Race and Sex in America* explores the role of women in the quest for equality. "Dawn," an account of Brewster's ironic postwar beginnings, interweaves the everyday rituals of the domestic arena with the community's destiny in order to underscore the close connection between private and public spheres and the incendiary potential of housewives and mothers. Cooking, cleaning, and mothering become hallmarks of the lives of women determined to safeguard their homes against the dangers looming in the larger society. The tendency on the part of bourgeoisie ideology to separate the domestic arena and its associated tasks from a public space is noticeably absent among the working-class poor. That Brewster's colored daughters perform housekeeping chores in their own homes as well as in those of whites affirms the continuation of the two worlds of work defining the black female reality during and after slavery (Jones 3–4). But the women of Brewster Place carry out domestic acts for the benefit of their own families and communities in ways that signal the political dimensions of home as "a site of resistance and liberation struggle" (hooks 43).

Among Brewster's colored daughters, the performance of ritual tasks associated with home offers a discursive link between stories, even as those everyday chores allow the reader to situate the domestic at the center of narrative action. The rituals of housekeeping begin in "Dawn," with its account of the community's ironic beginnings, and they continue throughout Brewster's history. Mattie Michael's commitment to housework reveals efforts on the part of Brewster's colored daughters to engage in the kind of service that is to result in an empowerment of the next generation. A chore that is as mundane as the preparation of oatmeal assumes ritual dimensions as Mattie becomes one with a timeless community of women whose attention to domestic tasks is to transform the home into a haven of security and tranquility (Rabuzzi 43–65). It is while washing dishes that Mattie contemplates Basil's growing apathy. He grows up, but because Mattie coddles him to the point where he is either unable or unwilling to make wise decisions or assume responsibility for his errant behavior, he lacks emotional maturity. The iridescent bubbles that burst in the sink symbolize Mattie's frustrated dreams for her wayward child. In a scene suggestive of the ways Mattie allows the maternal role to subsume her personal identity, the single mother is surprised when she sees her reflection in a windowpane. Mattie goes about her daily routine even after Basil abandons her as if nothing out of the ordinary has occurred. She prepares creamed chicken with rice—Basil's favorite meal—and while Mattie's cooking fails to prompt her son's return, her act becomes an expression of her resolve to maintain a home even in the face of uncertainty and loss.

It is within an inner-city domestic arena that Cora Lee, single mother of seven, glimpses her budding ability to bring about radical change, not such much for herself as for her children. Prior to her encounter with Abshu Ben-Jamal and Kiswana, the young woman's life is characterized by passivity and indifference; she is little more than a breeder whose role is to offer sexual gratification to the miscellaneous men who bring babies but no paycheck. Her relationships with men are short lived and at times characterized by domestic abuse. Once she meets the two community activists, however, the welfare mother begins to envision a better life. She thinks of her brother who has a post office job. Her daughter Maybelline could one day perform on stage like the actress at Abshu's production. When Sammy asks if Shakespeare is black, the young single mother responds, "Not yet," as if in anticipation of a bright future in the arts (127). Cleaning her disorderly apartment, mending her children's tattered clothing, and insisting that they complete their homework become sacrificial acts in the life of a politically awakened mother whose mission is to equip her children so that they can take their rightful places in the America's future.

Cora Lee's return home brings into sharp focus the limited options afforded black women in the city. She and her children go back to a clean, orderly apartment only to have one of her male friends let himself in with his own key. That the young woman submits to the whim of the anonymous male points to the difficulties of realizing the radically transformed future she envisions. When she next appears, it is in "The Block Party" and she is pregnant with her eighth child. It is noteworthy, however, that Cora Lee is first among Brewster's colored daughters to remove a brick from the wall (Fowler 48). In spite of her subjectivity to male desire, Cora Lee is capable of uniting with the other women in a challenge to amorphous power structure responsible for Brewster's creation.

Refiguring Borders, Dismantling Walls

Brewster's expanding borders serve as a site for the critique of externally imposed conceptions of space. If the brick wall circumscribing the community's bounds limits the achievements and aspirations of the working-class poor, then Mattie's vision of a unified community of women heralds the ability to transform the inner-city neighborhood into a place of renewal and fulfillment—a site where dreams can be realized. Without the wall and the limits that it portends, Brewster's dead-end street loses its stranglehold on the urban masses. In this regard, the tenants' association's cryptic slogan, "Today Brewster—Tomorrow America" (139), reiterates the collective desire on the part of Brewster's colored daughters to achieve an expanded sphere of influence that traverses the narrow boundaries delimiting the community and its residents.

Lucielia Louise Turner's narrative offers insight into the radically transformed social order that the novel signals. Ciel is the only woman in the housing project who is married, and her domestic life is fraught with turmoil. Instead of coming to terms with the fact that her husband Eugene is hopelessly irresponsible and incapable of accepting the responsibilities of manhood, she blames herself for their marital dysfunction. One of the couple's many arguments weighs heavily on Ciel's mind as she prepares dinner. Her inability to rid a pot of rice of its starch points to the futility underlying her efforts at achieving domestic bliss. Just as Ciel is unable to remove the starch from the pot, so too is she unable to silence the truth of her husband's instability.

It takes the tragedy of her daughter Serena's death to force Ciel into an awareness of her dilemma. Although Eugene shares his wife's grief, he lacks the strength necessary to console his wife during the couple's time of bereavement. Ciel is understandably devastated following Serena's death and the young woman reaches the lowest point of her life. It is at this point that Mattie emerges as a stalwart redemptive figure who ushers Ciel back from the depths of despair. Mattie bathes the grieving mother in a moving scene serving as the novel's emotional genesis:

> Ciel moaned. Mattie rocked. Propelled by the sound, Mattie rocked her out of that bed, out of that room, into a blue vastness underneath the sun and above time. She rocked her over Aegean seas so clean they shone like crystal, so clear the fresh blood of sacrificed babies torn from their mother's arms and given to Neptune could be seen like pink froth on the water. She rocked her on and on, past Dachau, where soul-gutted Jewish mothers swept their children's entrails off laboratory floors. They flew past the spilled brains of Senegalese infants whose mothers had dashed them on the wooden sides of slave ships. And she rocked on.
>
> She rocked her into her childhood and let her see murdered dreams. And she rocked her back, back into the womb, to the nadir of her hurt, and they found it—a slight silver splinter, embedded just below the surface of the skin. And Mattie rocked and pulled—and the splinter gave way, but its roots were deep, gigantic, ragged, and they tore up flesh with bits of fat and muscle tissue clinging to them. They left a huge hole, which was already starting to pus over, but Mattie was satisfied. It would heal. (103–4)

The scene affirms the oneness that Mattie and Ciel share with a timeless community of women who have lost children because of "the machinations of the patriarchy."[9] Figurations of a global network of grieving mothers point to an erasure of national boundaries in ways that presage a destabilization of artificial constructions of house and home. Mattie serves as the mediating figure occasioning a reversal of the psychologically destructive effects of female subjectivity within the institutions of the larger society. As a result of the elder woman's healing, redemptive presence, the bedroom and bath are transformed into sites of rejuvenation, places of rebirth existing outside the perimeters of a white, male gaze.

Naylor's fictional rendering of Ciel's apartment, and, indeed, Brewster itself, as a womblike nexus offering seemingly limitless opportunities for self-identity is not lost on the reader. Like Etta Mae Johnson, Ciel is reborn in the company of a transcendent female community. Mattie bathes the bereaved Ciel in a ritual act of healing, baptism, and initiation. The association that Joanne Gabbin's makes between the ritual of "a laying on of hands" in the tradition of black women's fiction and ancient practices involving folk healing permits the reader to situate the scene within an African Diasporic historiography.[10] Language exists at the junction of the circuitous network through which the women are obliged to pass. Ciel becomes the child that Mattie has lost; Mattie is the maternal vessel through which Ciel must journey before achieving new life. The voyage that both women make is therefore not only one that takes place within the recesses of a transcendent domestic space, but it is carried out in paradigmatic terms richly evocative of the acquisition of voice. Like that of the newborn, Ciel's plaintive moan is a prelinguistic code marking her entry into what Jenny Brantley describes as the realm of language and adult experience.[11] Whatever Ciel has endured, she will survive. In an expression of her evolutionary move toward a self not bound by patriarchal designations, the acquisition of agency apart from the vagaries of urban life, she appears in "The Block Party." Ciel has moved to San Francisco and is to be remarried. As if to signify Ciel's transformed self, the young woman's story concludes with an emphasis on rebirth and renewal: "And Ciel lay down and cried. But Mattie knew the tears would end. And she would sleep. And morning would come" (105).

Even though Brewster's condemnation is the expected end of a community that is destined to fail, emphasis on the institutional sites within the black community and the ritual acts associated with those spaces signal the ability of the folk to act independently of an urban bureaucracy. "Dusk" therefore foregrounds the performance of housekeeping tasks, linking the everyday moments of black women's lives with a mention of the community's fate so as to reveal the existence of a self-determining neighborhood existing in opposition to societal mandate:

> But the colored daughters of Brewster, spread over the canvas of time, still wake up with their dreams misted on the edge of a yawn. They get up and pin those dreams to wet laundry hung out to dry, they're mixed with a pinch of salt and thrown into pots of soup, and they're diapered around babies. They ebb and flow, ebb and flow, but never disappear. So Brewster still waits to die. (192; italicized in original)

In a reification of the domestic rituals that unify Brewster's colored daughters—washing clothes, preparing meals, and diapering babies—the novel ends with a portrait of a liminal community poised ambiguously both in and outside of time and space, en route to and forever defying its promised end.

2

Burning Down the Master's House:
Linden Hills

A House Is Not a Home

Like *The Women of Brewster Place*, *Linden Hills* examines the buried history of African Americans in terms of the creative, often clandestine, acts of rebellion arising from subaltern women. That these gestures of revolt in Naylor's second novel originate from the middle-class wife and mother calls into question notions of marriage not only as the sine qua non for personal fulfillment but also as the basis of an aristocratic social order. Women and, by implication, the feminine constitute the foundation of the masculine Empire figured by successive Luther Nedeed's reign over a posh suburban neighborhood. All that is required in an overthrow of this rule is women's awakening to the reality of a centuries-old subjugation and the power that gendered difference implies. Such an arousal occurs through a discovery of women's history and the revelation of the proactive subjectivity on the part of the subaltern. The novel thus chronicles the journey toward self-assertion that the middle-class wife makes once she recognizes her latent revolutionary potentiality.

Naylor's fictionalization of life among the suburban elite prompts her to make a distinction between the metaphor of house, a construct bound with established ideas of time, space, and identity, and that of home, a fluid configuration relevant to the border subject's ability to fashion a hybrid self unencumbered by essentialist designations. Iterations of the house-home dichotomy are resonant with feminist ideology and concepts about women's entrapment within what Sandra Gilbert and Susan Gubar describe as "the architecture—both the houses and the institutions—of patriarchy"

(85). They point out that, "[l]iterally confined to the house, figuratively confined to a single 'place,' enclosed in parlors and encased in texts, imprisoned in kitchens and enshrined in stanzas, women artists naturally found themselves describing dark interiors and confusing their sense that they were house-bound with their rebellion against being duty bound" (84). For the nineteenth-century woman writer struggling with issues of literary authority, dramatizations of enclosure and escape are so prevalent that they constitute a uniquely female tradition. Naylor's second novel offers a cultured, twentieth-century extension of that tradition with the account of Willa's spectacular ascent from her basement locus of exile. That she returns to the kitchen while carrying out housekeeping tasks places her in a long line of housewife-revolutionaries torn between a social identity as wife and mother and the public role of agent for social change. As the last woman in the Nedeed clan, Willa is to dismantle the master's house of patriarchal privilege and thereby disrupt the aristocratic ideology governing life in Linden Hills.

Of the various institutional sites figuring into the novel's fictional geography—the church, school, social clubs, and corporate arena—not one exists outside the purview of masculine control. Yet Naylor's concern is not so much with the public spaces defining a contemporary suburban landscape as with domestic space and its potential as either an extension of white, patriarchal authority or a locus for self-definition. Slavery offers a nineteenth-century nexus for an investigation of marriage and family under capitalist domination. Rumors that the first Luther Nedeed acquires the money used to purchase the land that later becomes Linden Hills by selling his octoroon wife and six children place the wealthy land baron in the dual role of husband and master. Successive generations of wives are valued solely in terms of their commodity status or procreative ability as breeders—a truth that places women in a situation not far removed from slavery.

The suppression of difference is the single most defining strategy underlying the elitist ideology among residents of Linden Hills.

As the omniscient narrator points out, "Linden Hills wasn't black; it was successful. The shining surface of their careers, brass railings, and cars hurt his eyes because it only reflected the bright nothing that was inside of them."[1] But Naylor's portrait of middle-class life reveals the difficulties associated with efforts to deny, contain, or circumscribe a cultured, gendered identity. Aspects of difference assert themselves at every turn, thereby disrupting a seemingly seamless story involving the search for a home divorced from agrarian associations. Much of *Linden Hills* involves Naylor's attempt to challenge established truth associated with a masculinist rendering of the history surrounding the Nedeed paternal dynasty. In this regard, the use of Lester Tilson and Willie K. Mason as guides allowing the reader access to the residents is a clever narrative strategy that offers insight into the complexities of life within the posh suburban district. Lester resides on the upper boundaries of Linden Hills with his mother and sister while Willie rents a room outside the area on Wayne Avenue. Lester is a high school graduate who publishes his poetry in the local newspaper. Willie, on the other hand, drops out of high school and memorizes his poetry rather than committing his verse to paper. Lester is known as "Baby Shit" because of his milky yellow skin tone, and Willie acquires the name "White Willie" despite his dark complexion (24).

That the two poet-guides both affirm and defy what their nicknames imply reveals a troubling of the dominant historiography within and against which central characters are to define themselves. In the fictional world Naylor constructs, names are unreliable signifiers of the self as the author attempts to subvert the identity politics underlying bourgeois capitalism. Both young men are poised on the brink of masculinity. The latent homoeroticism that Henry Louis Gates Jr. ascribes to the pair raises questions about constructions of black masculinity within the context of a society privileging a heterosexual norm.[2] Naylor's complex depiction of black male sexuality encourages a rethinking of the ways in which bourgeois capitalism attempts to proscribe the limits of a gendered self. If the portrait of the bond between Lester and Willie points to the existence of a counternarrative involving same sex relations, one finding expression in the relationship that Winston and David establish, then the bond between Willie and Willa constitutes the rupturing text that occasions the apocalyptic end of the Nedeed Empire.

Willie, who is closely aligned with the long-suppressed feminine principle, is Willa's alter ego, whose pre-Christmas sojourn through Linden Hills unearths the subterranean lives of women (see the interview with Naylor in the appendix). It is through him that Naylor scripts the feminine into what might otherwise have been a strictly masculine historiography and discursive space. The young poet enjoys a close relationship with a litany of female residents who struggle for self within a male-dominated setting. At one point he has a troubling dream in which he has no face. He continues to be disturbed by his experiences in Linden Hills and is unable to detach himself from Willa, his female counterpart: "But she was waiting for him, he felt that in his guts; he just had to fall asleep. Willie shuddered. Christ, now he was turning into a woman—he sounded like somebody's superstitious old aunt" (273). It is significant that he views Willa's image in a mirror prior to the destruction of the Nedeed mansion. As Willa makes her slow, deliberate journey back up the stairs leading to the kitchen, he gazes upon her disheveled visage in a symbolic, emancipating act that liberates him and, by extension, Willa herself from the oppressive institutions of the larger society. He and Lester then scale the fence circumscribing Linden Hills, hand-in-hand, in a symbolic gesture of male bonding that brings to mind the ending of Naylor's first novel with its representation of an exclusively female group gathered in order to dismantle the brick wall.

The account of the relationship between Norman and Ruth Anderson is one that offers a counterpoint to marriage and family under bourgeois domination. Much like her Old Testament precursor, Ruth is "a symbol of divine love" whose filial loyalty prompts her to stay in a distressed marriage.[3] The omniscient narrator reminds the reader that despite its meager furnishings, the Andersons' garden apartment "*was* a home with its bare wood floors, dusted and polished, and with the three pieces of furniture that sat in three large rooms: one sofa in the living room, one kitchenette set with plastic-bottomed chairs on uncertain chrome legs, one bed" (33). It is within the perimeters of the Andersons' egalitarian marriage that established gender roles lose all validity. Norman assumes the role of nurturer and care giver when he tends to his ailing wife, thereby adopting a traditionally feminine role. Ruth is no less devoted to her husband. His mysterious illness, which Virginia Fowler rightly associates with the urge toward whiteness, prompts the uncontrollable rages that cause him to destroy the couple's furnishings (74). Over the years Ruth refuses to replace their furniture, signaling her realization that material possessions are not a prerequisite for personal happiness. Lester and Willie are immediately at ease in the couple's presence. In an act of communal sharing, when the four drink coffee from Styrofoam cups, it is as if the cups and their content are transformed into fine china and cognac. The code of male dominance that governs life in aristocratic Linden Hills is rendered null and void when Norman concedes, "Love rules in this house ..." (38).

While the Andersons' relationship serves as a counterpoint to marriage among Linden Hills elite, Laurel DuMont's story brings into sharp focus the dangers associated with a life divorced from an agrarian past and its sustaining traditions. The young woman achieves an unparalleled level of success when she graduates from Berkeley and rises to a management level position in the corporate world. Marriage to the first African American district attorney in Wayne County is the crowning achievement for the aspiring woman. What she discovers is that material gain fails to fill the inner void engulfing her life. Emblematic of the vacuum created as a result of the pursuit of the American Dream, Laurel's malaise is evident with the growing emotional distance between herself and Howard: "The couple had everything; she had to believe that because everyone told her so. And with so much in that house, they didn't miss each other as they both stumbled on their way up, not realizing that their stairways weren't strictly parallel. Slowly, deceptively, the steps slanted until the couple's fingertips could just barely meet across the chasm" (232). The stairway is a liminal space that indicates the prescribed identities Naylor's characters must adopt in their move up the socioeconomic ladder. By virtue of the pursuit of material success, Linden Hills residents are compelled to forfeit their sense of self. This is the truth that Winston learns when he is forced to abandon his relationship with longtime lover David. The upwardly mobile attorney must choose between fidelity to his bond with his gay comrade and marriage to Cassandra. That Winston elects to sever ties with David suggests the extent to which the young attorney has internalized the larger society's ideals.

For Laurel, the ascent up the corporate ladder occasions a loss of self when she surrenders her cultural moorings in the pursuit of money, status, and power. As if to remind the young woman of her marginal status, Luther evicts her once he learns of the DuMonts' impending divorce. That Laurel's story is told in retrospect from her grandmother Roberta's point of view serves to situate home within the context of a folk epistemology involving vernacular accounts of survival in the face of seemingly insurmountable odds. Like Mamie Tilson, whose timeless wisdom prompts her to warn against the forfeiture of cultural memory in the quest for wealth, Roberta offers sage advice concerning black endurance in contemporary America. The aged woman's connection with an agrarian South, evidenced by her down-home cooking, stories about Br'er Fox and Br'er Rabbit, and mother wit, ground her in an insistently maternal reality that exists outside the purview of the Nedeed paternal dynasty. The most compelling lesson that she imparts to her distressed granddaughter involves the blues as a locus of female empowerment: "It ain't a music that speaks to your body like that rock music of these kids. But it speaks to a place they ain't got no name for yet, where you supposed to be at home. Open up that place, child. 'Cause if you don't, there ain't never gonna be no peace—with the love in your life or the hurt" (236). Roberta's words echo a similar pronouncement on the part of Mamie Tilson, whose wise counsel Lester recounts in a conversation with Willie:

> She would often say, "Child, there's gonna come a time when you'll look at the world and not know what the blazes is going on. Somebody'll be calling you their father, their husband their boss—whatever. And it can get confusing, trying to sort all that out, and you can lose yourself in other people's minds. You can forget what you really want and believe. So you keep that mirror and when it's crazy *outside,* you look inside and you'll always know exactly where you are and what you are. And you call that peace." Ya know, White? (59)

The wisdom encoded in the women's advice reveals the failure on the part of white-dominated institutions in offering a sense of well-being necessary in contemporary America. In order to find fulfill-ment, individuals must therefore challenge the false self-image that the larger society presents and forge an identity existing apart from prescriptive ideas of blackness. Collectively, the elder women posit home as an unnamed, unmapped space—a site located outside fixed bounds—involving freedom from artificial restraint. In this re-gard, their sage words offer a starting point for Laurel's redemption, an unscripted map leading to the young woman's recovery. That Laurel chooses the classic strains of Gustav Mahler and Bach over the earthy lyrics of Bessie Smith or Billie Holiday reveals her dis-tance from the folk sensibility that has nurtured her grandmother. Not surprisingly, Laurel never achieves the tranquility and fortitude that characterizes Roberta's life, and the young woman's search for fulfillment culminates with suicide.

In her abandonment of cultural memory, the successful cor-porate executive has also left behind her grounding in a reality that offers the key to her salvation. Reversing the geographic movement underlying the Great Migration, Laurel returns to her grandmother's rural Georgia residence in a last opportunity for redemption. Yet the psychological distance from her grandmother's vibrant heritage prevents her from reconnecting with the past. From her Westernized perspective, Roberta's home is little more than a shack, a place bereft of any nurturing, sustaining associations. Much like the Europeanized Jadine Childs in Toni Morrison's *Tar Baby,* or the college-educated Dee in Alice Walker's "Everyday Use," Laurel is the colonized subject who has abandoned the traditions and ritual practices that hold the key to her deliverance.

Once she returns to Linden Hills, Laurel tries in vain to transform the twelve-room Tudor-style mansion she shared with her husband into the space she associates with home. Her failed efforts at renovating the expansive residence suggest her unwillingness or inability to make a critical distinction between house and home. In commenting on Laurel's dilemma, Naylor points out that she identifies not so much with Willa as with Laurel, who "forgets where home is."[4] Sadly, Laurel remains entrapped within the larger society and its appraisals. Without the emotional buffer that an agrarian past would offer, she is engulfed by despair. Her climb up the corporate ladder ends tragically with a suicidal plunge into a swimming pool.

Good Housekeeping and Other Misnomers

Whereas *The Women of Brewster Place* culminates with Mattie Michael's dream of an empowered group of inner-city women who dismantle a brick wall, narrative action in Naylor's second novel foregrounds an event that is similarly as incendiary: Willa's discovery of the documents connecting her with the maternal predecessors who find themselves subjected to the tyrannical behavior of Luther Nedeed. Through the papers she unearths, the beleaguered housewife comes to realize the "shared domestic tragedies" linking her life with that of other Nedeed wives (Fowler 108). Equally as important in an understanding of spaces of resistance in Naylor's evolving canon is the role Willa assumes as a decoder of the information that she finds. The miscellaneous documents she finds— photographs, cookbooks, and journal entries—constitute a "text" attesting to women's fledgling attempts at authorship within the confines of a male-dominated setting. The documents Willa reads bear a close resemblance to the often private, gendered forms of expression figuring into texts by Jane Austen, Charlotte Perkins Gilman, the Brontës, and Emily Dickinson—precursor works likely inspiring Naylor and other women writers. Discovering the documents serves as a catalyst for Willa's escape from the basement of the Nedeed mansion in ways that suggest a connection between Naylor's housewife and female protagonists in earlier writing. Not only that, but Naylor's account of the metamorphosis that Willa undergoes as a result of reading the texts that her maternal forebears leave behind also sheds light on the uniquely cultured, gendered quest for literary authority on the part of the black female writer.

The canonical story embedded in the documents that the Nedeed wives author point to figurations of the margins as a site of dynamic potentiality so as to distinguish Willa's situation from that of white female protagonists in texts by nineteenth-century women writers. The miscellaneous documents that the Nedeed wives produce bear witness to fledgling efforts toward the achievement of literary authority in a society where black women are doubly oppressed. Willie, whose preference for oral poetry aligns him with the folk tradition of Jupiter Hammon, laments the fact that Linden Hills has not produced a writer whose stature rivals that of Shakespeare. His observations regarding black creative expression bring to mind Alice Walker's discussion of the material conditions surrounding black female expressivity in her landmark essay "In Search of Our Mothers' Gardens." Willie rents a room on the outskirts of the wealthy neighborhood, without the luxury of owning his own place, as if to challenge the prerequisites for creative expression that Virginia Wolfe outlines in *A Room of One's Own*. But it is Willie who is charged with the task of rendering an inclusive history of the upper-middle-class neighborhood—one that takes into account the hidden lives of women. His complex subjectivity makes him an apt candidate for telling the story of the Nedeed wives.

The documents that the Nedeed wives author reveal a suppressed history of female resistance, with the domestic arena serving as ritual grounds for rebellion against race, class, and gender oppression. The marriage between Luther I and Luwana Packerville sheds light on the dilemma successive generations of women face as they attempt to define themselves within and against the institutions of the dominant society. An ex-slave, Luwana looks forward to marriage and the move north, but her happiness is short lived when matrimony occasions a recapitulation of the bondage the young woman hoped to escape. Luther is as unrelenting in his authoritative rule over her when he elects to liberate his son while maintaining ownership of Luwana. The distressed woman reveals the nature of her dilemma in ways that associate marriage with slavery: "O Blessed Saviour, can it be that I have only exchanged one master for another? Can it be that the innocent scribblings I sought only to hide from a husband's amused contempt are now the diary of a slave?" (117). Luwana's sense of alienation is heightened not only because of her displacement from Tupelo, Mississippi, but also as a result of her isolation from black and white women in the North. Upon learning of a woman in Tennessee who is hanged for poisoning her master's soup, Luther hires a housekeeper to cook and wash, thereby increasing Luwana's marginality. Banishment of his wife to a basement is the penultimate repressive act on the part of a despot intent on quelling the perceived threat that the subaltern wife presents.

Unlike Brewster's colored daughters, who forge empowering bonds of sisterhood that transform the failing community into a comforting safe haven, Luwana leads a solitary life unrelieved by acceptance within a community of women. Her only solace is in the journal entries she pens as she writes about her troubles. It is in the writing of those entries that the woman manifests a quest for autonomy that unites her with marginalized women in struggle, slave and free. Strategically placed within the pages of her Bible, Luwana's "innocent scribblings" challenge scriptural authority. Her writing is thus no less threatening than the anonymous slave woman's retaliatory act against a slave master. Intensely political in their revelation of the bourgeois wife's plight, those entries function as a counterhegemonic discourse indicative of Luwana's propensity to speak from the margins (hooks 38).

Subsequent Nedeed wives are likewise inclined to employ stratagems serving as retaliatory acts directed toward the larger society and restraining definitions of the female self, thereby linking these women with the radical lineage of Nat Turner, Denmark Vesey, and Marcus Garvey—"madmen" who, according to Luther I, pose a threat to the stability of the Nedeed paternal dynasty (11). Yet Naylor is careful to highlight the gendered dimensions of black insurgence. The acts of rebellion on the part of the Nedeed wives are private and covert in nature. An obsession with food mirrors Evelyn Creton's growing despondence when she records the purchase of grocery items with fanatical attention to detail. Later, she develops an eating disorder that prompts her to overindulge then purge herself. Suicide marks the end of her efforts to regain her husband's affection. Even though her recollection of Mama Day's herbal potions designed to serve as an aphrodisiac indicate the residual presence of folk beliefs in the North, Evelyn continues to define herself in terms of the politics of cultural representation present in white America.

A series of photographs register the loss of self Priscilla McGuire's experiences as a consequence of marriage and motherhood. The once-independent woman appearing in an early photograph with a cigarette in her hand figures in subsequent pictures as diminishing into the shadow of her husband and son. But the last picture, which includes a faceless image of the housewife along with her husband and son, is one onto which she inscribes "me," in a radical act of self-affirmation that belies notions of female subordination within a masculinist social order (249).

Naylor's second novel posits the bourgeois marriage as grounds for gestures of revolt directed toward the larger society and its stifling dictates. The collective experiences of the Nedeed wives underscore the potentially incendiary dimensions of the domestic arena as a site of empowerment for dispossessed women across time and space. Through the presence of miscellaneous documents attesting to the wives' struggle for autonomy, Naylor points to the existence of a counterhegemonic discourse or alternate narrative— one that undermines the authority ascribed to Daniel Braithwaite's twelve-volume chronicle of Linden Hills. Under the auspices of Luther Nedeed, Braithwaite undertakes the business of recording events transpiring in the upper-middle-class neighborhood. But his staunchly objective perspective prompts him to exclude the subterranean experiences of individuals living outside of the social mainstream. Despite his claims of offering "the whole story," the Fisk-educated historian relies solely on extant records in compiling his documents (263). Nor does he fulfill his moral obligation to intervene in residents' headlong plunge into a capitalist hell. Naylor refers to him as being "the worse type of academic you could have: someone who could go through life sapping knowledge."[5] When Lester asks whether the scholar might use knowledge in order to save individuals from a tragic end, Braithwaite tells Lester and Willie, "Luther knows and I know that I can only hope to record that knowledge, not rectify it" (262). He therefore evinces a scholarly detachment that makes him culpable in the residents' fate.

Stairways, Entrances, and Transitional Sites

It is not Braithwaite but Willie, the gutsy, outspoken folk poet, who is to render a revised, comprehensive chronicle of Linden Hills—one that takes into account the buried history of black women. Because of his close association with individuals existing on the margins,

Willie is to tell *her* story, an inclusive narrative revealing the particular experiences of the middle-class wife. It is within the larger discursive framework of the documents that the Nedeed wives author that the reader must situate the account of Willa's ascent from the basement. In much the same way that women during and after slavery have made their presence known by exercising agency apart from the dominant society, so too does Willa follow a trajectory leading to female autonomy and self-definition. In other words, Willa must strike a balance between the traditional role of wife and mother, on the one hand, and the revolutionary activism necessary in dismantling the master's house of female subjugation, on the other. By far the most salient threat to the autonomy women seek is the idea of heterosexual normativity, and Luther goes to extreme lengths in order to repress all evidence of a departure from what Kimberly Costino describes as the compulsory heterosexuality governing life in Linden Hills.[6] That Willa bears not only a white son but also one who resembles his mother offers evidence of the gendered history of subaltern women in the Nedeed dynasty. Her alleged infidelity, with overtones of the wife's sexual autonomy, reifies the feminine in ways that presage a destabilization of the identity politics governing middle-class life.[7] Sinclair, who remains unnamed throughout much of the novel, functions as a rupturing text, a sign, or the unscripted signifying difference undermining a masculinist discourse or the law of the father. Luther's assertion of his wife's purported adultery occurs in terms of an awakening to the feminine:

> He could see the amber flecks in the heavily lashed eyes,
> the tiny scar on the right side of her lips. The long neck, small
> breasts, thick waist. Woman. She became a constant irritant
> to Luther, who now turned her presence over in his mind
> several times a day. Somewhere inside of her there must be a
> deep flaw or she wouldn't have been capable of such treach-
> ery. Everything she owned he had given—even her name—

and she had thanked him with this? The irritation began to fester in his mind and he knew he had to remove it or go insane. He could throw her out tomorrow; there wasn't a court in this country that would deny him that right, but no one in his family had ever gotten divorced. And she had to learn why she was brought to Tupelo Drive. Obviously, he had allowed a whore into his home but he would turn her into a wife. (19)

In banishing his wife and son to the basement, Luther intends to curtail the transgressive sexuality that Willa's alleged adultery implies. But he sets the stage for his demise when he attempts to impose the polarized identities delimiting his wife's achievement. The dictatorial husband fails to recognize that Linden Hills is a gendered space that mediates against Luther's colonialist enterprise and notions of male dominance. Naylor mentions the relationship between self and women's perceptions of space and how space "was to be a metaphor for that middle-class woman's married existence [as] she was shoved into that basement."[8] Representations of the middle-class neighborhood as a "V-shaped section of land" with "boundaries [that] contracted and expanded over the years to include no one, and then practically everyone in Wayne County" bring to mind figurations of home as a womblike matrix, a series of crisscrossing networks allowing for unlimited movement (1). It is in the basement, a space reserved for the subaltern, that Willa encounters a timeless community of maternal foremothers united by their entrapment within and creative response to patriarchal control. The housewife not only becomes acquainted with the women's individual and collective histories but also acknowledges the ways in which her personal narrative bears a connection with those of her female predecessors. Willa is reborn within the recesses of the domestic space as she journeys toward the identity she has long been denied. Virginia Fowler is correct in the observation that Willa's agency increases as the housewife reads the documents that the

Nedeed maternal ancestors author (84). Willa undergoes a transformation with ritual overtones—one that prompts her to distance herself from the prescribed roles she has assumed.

At first the subaltern housewife defines herself exclusively within the context of a traditional role. In a scene revealing of the liminal state through which Willa must pass as she journeys toward self-identity, Naylor allows the woman to see herself in a cook pot. Willa must disassociate herself from the myriad images of black femininity that the larger society presents before she can discover who she is. Naylor's oppressed housewife experiences a major turning point in her evolutionary growth when she comes to realize the part she plays in her subjugation: "She was sitting there now, filthy, cold, and hungry, because she, Willa Prescott Nedeed, had walked down twelve concrete steps. And since that was the truth— the pure, irreducible truth—whenever she was good and ready, she could walk back up" (282).

Willa's housekeeping occurs in terms suggestive of the agency she exercises apart from the mandates of her dictatorial husband. The stairway that she ascends, like those figuring into Winston and Cassandra's wedding and the ones referenced in a description of Laurel Dumont's climb up the corporate ladder, serves as a transitional site revealing the fixed polarities of the hierarchal identities available to black women. Reminiscent of self-help programs, the twelve steps that she climbs point to Willa's mediation between established roles. She is the "queen amidst a horde of army ants" who must challenge the line of fathers present in the Nedeed family (297). After organizing the basement, Willa proceeds up the stairs leading to the kitchen and den.

Much to Naylor's dismay, Willa elects to forgo the revolutionary role that her working-class counterparts adopt in the author's first novel and reclaim a subordinate place as housewife.[9] Her frenzied attention to the everyday tasks associated with hearth and home is a private undertaking divorced from community empowerment or uplift. Death is the inevitable consequence of her inability to carry out her detachment from a masculine social order. Critics tend to interpret the novel's rather bizarre, unresolved ending as a defeat for the beleaguered housewife and mother.[10] But Willa's ascent can be understood within the framework of her conjoined relationship with Willie. Although Willa does not succeed at escaping the house or executing vengeance on Luther, her ascent is directly responsible for the destruction of the Nedeed Empire. She surrenders her life in what Christopher Okonkwo rightly describes as a messianic act that brings an end to the Nedeed paternal dynasty (117–31). Willie, an emerging artist and cultural historian who is closely aligned with the folk, serves as Willa's dark double—the medium through which her story and, by extension, that of the Nedeed wives is to be retold. As he composes his 666th poem, not only is he to situate Willa into what otherwise might have been a strictly masculine chronicle of Linden Hills, but he will offer a complete story of the neighborhood—one that reflects the uniquely cultured, gendered experiences of black women. In other words, Willie, the novel's hyper-feminized male, furthers the agency that his female counterpart began. Along with Luther and Sinclair, Willa perishes in the fire destroying the Nedeed mansion. Willie and Lester scale the fence demarcating Linden Hills, crossing over imposed boundaries in the journey toward the promising future that the new year heralds.

Linden Hills represents Naylor's move toward inscribing a utopian domestic space not bound by patriarchy or bourgeois capitalism. Because the Nedeed mansion is a construct evolving out of a masculinist order, it cannot be reconfigured; instead, the master's house must be dismantled. One awakened woman—a housewife—serves as a catalyst, not of a New World Order but of the end of an old one, and her life's story becomes the stuff of legend and lore. Naylor's second novel thus points to a destabilization of received notions of hearth and home, even as it paves the way for the patently female household emerging in *Mama Day.*

3

Finding Peace in the Middle: *Mama Day*

Everybody's Mama, Nobody's Slave:
Reinscribing the Legend of Sapphira Wade

Since her appearance in Gloria Naylor's *Mama Day*, Sapphira Wade has been the unwitting subject of varied and, at times, competing critical readings drawn from African as well as European points of view. Dorothy Perry Thompson regards the island matriarch as "the conflation of the need for a new woman-centered spirituality and ancient African ancestor worship."[1] Susan Meisenhelder refers to her as "Naylor's ideal black woman."[2] More recently, in an interrogation of the Africana mythological and spiritual nexus out of which Sapphira evolves, Teresa Washington suggests the figure as "the tutelary Orisha of Willow Springs and the center around which the text and textual lives revolve and evolve" (116–17). The range of critical perspectives brought to bear upon the Willow Springs matriarch enhances her mystique even as it purports to illuminate Sapphira and the novel that has immortalized her. Viewing her is much like gazing at an object through a kaleidoscopic lens: She remains static but is seemingly ever changing, defying reductive attempts at naming, labeling, and, hence, circumscription. Her presence lends a rich complexity to the novel—a work that is as intricate as the double-ring quilt pattern that Miranda and Abigail stitch—and she draws the reader into the text, engaging us in the myth making surrounding Willow Springs' most famous, or, more aptly, infamous, resident.

If there is one aspect of *Mama Day* that critics agree upon, it has to do with the relative dimensions of truth in a novel evolving out of the fluid lore emanating from Sea Island culture. Truth is never fixed; rather, like Sapphira herself, objective reality is as dynamic as the uncertain boundaries demarcating the Willow Springs community. The story of the island matriarch "ain't about right or wrong, truth or lies," the communal narrator reminds the reader.[3] Mama Day points out that "everybody wants to be right in a world where ain't no right or wrong to be found" (230). She tells George, prior to his journey to the chicken coop, that "ain't about a right way or wrong way—just two ways" (295). Finally, after George's untimely death, Cocoa concedes regarding their courtship and marriage, "[T]here are just too many sides to the whole story" (311). The vibrant lore of the indigenous population subverts predetermined meaning encoded in institutionalized discourse, linguistic fact, or, to interject a term especially germane to Naylor's authorial strategy, master narrative of white, patriarchal dominance. Established truth becomes a fiction at the hands of the author who, in the case of Naylor's imaginative rendering of the legend of Sapphira Wade, privileges cultural memory as a site of resistance against the imposition of colonial rule. In Naylor's fictional cosmology as in oral tradition, the power to recall is an enabling mnemonic practice among those denied access to the written word and printed text. Remembering thus allows for the creation of an alternate reality, a counterhegemonic discourse that critiques, undermines, and subverts cultural paradigms of the dominant society.

Willow Springs closely resembles what Homi Bhabha describes as a Third Space of cultural fluidity and transnational identity (*The Location of Culture*). The restrictive bounds circumscribing the upper-middle-class neighborhood in *Linden Hills* give way to a uniquely maternal island paradise that defies geographic limits. An examination of *Mama Day*'s intermediate locale not only sheds light on the postcolonial search for a utopian home that transcends artificially imposed boundaries but also encourages the reader to foreground that quest within the larger geographic and discursive framework of the middle passage. Naylor's reliance upon a range of vernacular sources results in the creation of a multifaceted text in which oral lore encodes the circuitous route to home.

If there is a persona that is emblematic of this journey, it is the trickster, a transatlantic figure whose subtle modus operandi is to disrupt and subvert. Susan Meisenhelder, Lindsey Tucker, Teresa Washington, and Daphne Lamothe have read Sapphira, Miranda, and even Willow Springs residents as figurations of the elusive folkloric persona.[4] What remains to be done in an interrogation of *Mama Day,* Naylor's critically most acclaimed work and a novel demonstrating her dependence upon myth making, word play, masking, code switching, and modes of disruption and deception—in short, the narrative approach that has catapulted her into the vanguard of late-twentieth-century letters—is an investigation of trickster lore and its implications in terms of spaces of resistance. Naylor's third novel is what Henry Louis Gates Jr. would refer to as a "speakerly text" in the tradition of Zora Neale Hurston's *Their Eyes Were Watching God,* a classic text of the black woman's experience (*The Signifying Monkey*). In writing *Mama Day,* Naylor relies not only upon Hurston's spirit, but also her politics regarding the speech of the folk.[5] The communal voice that introduces the reader to Willow Springs is, much like the narrator in Hurston's classic novel, "a hybrid character, a character who, as Gates points out, is neither the novel's protagonist nor the text's disembodied narrator" (xxvi). In executing the improvisational play that allows her to mediate between multiple and, at times, competing voices, narratives, and texts, Naylor employs a method recalling that of turn-of-the-century local colorist Charles W. Chesnutt, whose ingenious plantation tales of conjuration permit Uncle Julius to turn the tables on a smug white northern businessman and wife. Chesnutt, like Uncle Julius, dons a mask that grants him space to privilege once-marginalized African spiritual and mythological systems in addressing a radical tale of black empowerment and self-determination to an unsuspecting predominantly white readership. Commenting on *The Conjure Woman,* Julie B. Farwell offers insight into the trickster and its implications for literary criticism when she says, "Chesnutt challenges the jurisdiction of white discourse over black expressive modes, and offers alternative African American models of authority in conjure and signifying."[6]

Naylor reinscribes many of the same African cultural practices that brought Chesnutt wide critical acclaim. Yet her adaptation of Africanisms such as conjure, magic, and root working, as Lindsey Tucker fittingly demonstrates in "Recovering the Conjure Woman: Texts and Contexts in Gloria Naylor's *Mama Day*," is not without complication and dissonance.[7] Naylor lends a decidedly gendered, postcolonial voice to the saga of black resistance as the author relies upon subversion and disruption in the creation of an alternate reality that challenges the discourses of the larger society. The legend of Sapphira Wades serves as a locus for interrogating Naylor's authorial stratagem. As if to align her with rebellious slaves throughout the transatlantic world, the island matriarch is of pure African stock. Scholars such as Patricia Jones-Jackson have noted that the Sea Islanders are from the Congo-Angola region in Africa where the most rebellious blacks originated (132–33). Much like the recklessly defiant African prince in William Melvin Kelley's *A Different Drummer,* whose escape from a slave market inspires his descendant Tucker Caliban to spread salt on the land, burn down the family house, and journey north, she is one in a line of dark-complexioned black figures whose presence mediates between Africa and the West. Included in this pantheon are the fictional characters Josh Green in Chesnutt's *Marrow of Tradition,* Tea Cake in Zora Neale Hurston's *Their Eyes Were Watching God,* Son in Toni Morrison's *Tar Baby,* and Tadpole in Gayl Jones's *Corregidora.* Stories detailing her journey back to Africa foreground accounts of the black flight to freedom in ways that lift her out of the realm of history and onto a mythic, supernatural plane.

But the novel not only reveals the ways in which Naylor rewrites historical moments involving the middle passage, slavery, and urban migration, it unveils the ways she upsets the identity politics that would ascribe a biological determinant to the act of black insurgence. Sapphira is, by all accounts, at once "satin black," "biscuit cream," *and* "red as Georgia clay" (4). By nature, she is a woman whose shifting subjectivities place her outside the bounds of the Western empiricism of both Reema's college-educated son and the dislocated urbanite George Andrews. Figurations of the island matriarch bring to mind the titular character in Sherley Anne Williams's *Dessa Rose,* whose intriguing story of the quest for freedom through flight defies attempts at inscription on the part of the ambitious yet inept historiographer Adam Nehemiah. By her own account, the fugitive slave is "too light for Mist's and not light enough for Masa.'"[8] As is the case with Dessa Rose, a trickster in her own right whose love affair with Kaine assumes mythic dimensions, an examination of the various texts reconstructing Sapphira's life serve to center narrative action within the perimeters of domestic space or home—one that exists only in cultural memory—which becomes a locus for the critique of predetermined racial and gender roles and colonialist myths inscribing white male dominance and female subservience.

Naylor flips the script on such myths with the account of Willow Springs' origins. In a reworking of the Genesis story of the Creation, the island matriarch is pitted against God in a contest for power, authority, and influence:

> The island got spit out from the mouth of God, and when it
> fell to the earth it brought along an army of stars. He tried
> to reach down and scoop them back up, and found Himself
> shaking hands with the greatest conjure woman on earth.
> "Leave 'em here, Lord," she said. "I ain't got nothing but these
> poor black hands to guide my people, but I can lead on with
> light." (110)

In *Mules and Men,* Zora Neale Hurston rightly points out that in folklore God is often a figure for white authority (254). Through the use of spiritual power linked with the feminine, or what Teresa

Washington refers to as aje, a "vastly influential power that is in-clined toward paradox and multiplicity," Sapphira not only reverses the balance of power between herself and a masculine deity but also turns the tables on a slaveholding aristocracy (13–14). Conjure al-lows the island matriarch to maintain a spiritual connection with Africa and enjoy an expanded sphere of influence outside both house and field. She wrests control over the land that later becomes Wil-low Springs, paving the way for the unprecedented self-sufficiency island residents inherit.

Even though Sapphira attains extraordinary sovereignty through her spiritual and feminine powers, a juxtaposition of the Creation myth detailing the island's beginnings with the ambigui-ties of Sapphira's identity encourages the reader to rethink the lim-its of unrestrained female autonomy. The terms inscribed on the bill of sale documenting Wade's alleged purchase of Sapphira cast doubt on her true self, as the woman referenced in the document merely answers to the name Sapphira. Furthering this uncertainty, the communal narrator points out that "Sapphira don't live in the part of our memory we can use to form words" and " . . . the name Sapphira Wade is never breathed out of a single mouth in Willow Springs" (4). Mama Day tells George that Wade is "calling and call-ing the name that nobody knows" (206). George reminds Cocoa when the couple visits the other place, "But legend or no, for you that wasn't her name" (248). It is not until the search for Cocoa's cure is underway that Mama Day encounters Sapphira in a dream. Like Williams in her revisionist account of black insurgency, Naylor uses names or naming in order to disrupt the dominant histori-ography within and against which characters are defined. Cocoa, who is light skinned and feels out of place among brown-skinned island women, is at once Cocoa, Ophelia, and Baby Girl—a com-posite of her myriad subjectivities. The facts of her checkered family history, George asserts, "were as clear as your complexion" (225). Only within the boundaries of Willow Springs does she realize the cultural hybridity that Homi Bhabha ascribes to the postcolonial subject whose identity owes no allegiance to singularly constructed notions of self (4). Outside of Willow Springs, she is fragmented, a victim of the psychologically divisive effects of life in the West.

Teresa Washington suggests the sassy, outspoken Sapphire of *Amos 'n' Andy* fame as a possible precursor for the mythical island foremother (120). Although illuminating in terms of Naylor's indebtedness to likely antecedent sources, such an explanation obscures the subtle verbal play underlying Naylor's authorial practice. Equally as viable a source for the Willow Springs matriarch is the biblical account of Sapphira, the compliant wife in Acts who lies to the Apostle Peter about the sale of land. Death is the price for the biblical Sapphira's complicity in her husband's deception. A combination of these two opposing models of womanhood—rebellion and submission—offers a balanced portrait of the black female subject in ways that offer an enriching interpretation of Sapphira and her relations with Bascombe Wade. Patricia Hill-Collins identifies black women's diverse reaction to being objectified as "the other" as a core theme in black feminist thought and explores the ways in which African American women writers challenge negative, controlling images (67–90). One method of countering such destructive representations is by creating multifaceted female characters that defy positive categorization or the tendency toward essentialism on the part of the larger society. It is this method that informs Naylor's creation of Sapphira and the island matriarch's female descendants, whose complicated selves owe no allegiance to singularly constructed ideas of time, space, or identity.

Crossing Over to "The Other Place"

With a history rooted in cultural hybridity and a reification of self-determining women who achieve semidivine stature, Willow Springs presents itself, at least on a superficial level, as home—a site of healing and renewal where parts torn as a result of the transatlantic journey are restored (Gilroy). Cocoa tells the reader regarding her ritual return to the island, "The rest of me—the whole of me—was here" (176). In Naylor's fourth novel, *Bailey's Café*, such a place is accessible only through the blues and finds fullest expression within the recesses of Eve's ambiguous boardinghouse/bordello, a safe haven for postwar global misfits. The South is figured as an ancestral home in much of African American oral and written discourse. Scholar bell hooks speaks of the journey to her grandmother's southern residence using distinctly political terms:

> Historically, black women have resisted white supremacist domination by working to establish homeplace. It does not matter that sexism assigned them this role. It is more important that they took this conventional role and expanded it to include caring for one another, for children, for black men, in ways that elevated our spirits, that kept us from despair, that taught some of us to be revolutionaries able to struggle for freedom. (44)

Home, which is nuanced in such a way as to invoke the postcolonial subject's conflicted connection with nationhood, the past, and ancestral roots, is rendered in elliptical fashion through Willow Springs' communal voice: "Home. Folks call it different things, think of it in different ways. For Cocoa it's being around living mirrors with the power to show a woman that she's still carrying scarred knees, a runny nose, and socks that get walked down into the heels of her shoes" (48). The gospel song "Precious Lord, Take My Hand," which George and his drunken companions intone following the all-male card game, a ritual event forging a tenuous bond between George and masculine island residents, foregrounds the search for ancestral beginnings among a global association of individuals in transit between nations, cultures, and geographies, those whom Homi Bhabha refers to as the "unhomely" (9–18). Yet the island is not, as Daphne Lamothe points out, the ancestral or familial home that the cosmopolitan orphan George Andrews never knew, nor is it the sanctuary that Cocoa attempts to re-create through her annual migratory journey back to Willow Springs, the placement of herbs and handmade sweet-grass baskets in her New York apartment, or her ill-fated hair-braiding session with Ruby.[9] Ruby's conjuring of Cocoa, the premature death of Little Caesar, and the violent storm that disrupts the island community offer evidence of a dark side to the paradise George invokes once he and Cocoa cross over to Willow Springs. Abigail might refer to the citified engineer affectionately as her child, but George is still an interloper who is reluctant to embrace the islanders and their folkways.

Nowhere is the narrative complication of home more evident than in the marriage between Wade and Sapphira, whose relationship serves as a nineteenth-century nexus for an understanding of the marriage between George and Cocoa. George wishes to rewrite the tense Day family history involving irreconcilable tension between men and women. The author's clever reinscription of the legend of Sapphira Wade suggests master-slave liaisons as fertile historic ground for an interrogation of plantation myths current in the nineteenth-century South and the residual effects of those myths in contemporary male-female relations. The three prefatory documents included at the beginning of the novel offer a link with the slave narrative genre, but here again Naylor troubles the veracity of the facts inscribed in written discourse through a focus on community lore. There is a map detailing the location of Willow Springs. That Reema's son wishes to put the island on the map indicates the ways in which his Western rational thinking renders him incapable of seeing what is otherwise readily apparent. George is frustrated by his inability to locate Willow Springs on his map. Virginia Fowler is accurate in her assertion that "the playful map in front of the novel functions on one level certainly as a kind of joke" (94). Beyond that, and consistent with the novel's vernacular roots in the folktale, the confusion surrounding the exact geographic location of the island paradise points to Naylor's role in subverting fixed historiography when she turns the tables on both Reema's college-trained son and the literal-minded engineer George Andrews. Cocoa announces, once she and George cross over to Willow Springs, "Your maps were no good here" (177).

The terms inscribed on the bill of sale documenting Wade's alleged purchase of Sapphira indicate that she "is half prime, inflicted with sullenness and entertains a bilious nature, having resisted under reasonable chastisement the performance of field or domestic labour." Even though the document is to authenticate Wade's ownership of Sapphira, the legend and lore surrounding Sapphira's life underscores the folly of attempts on the part of Wade and, by implication, anyone to possess, contain, or delineate the black subject. In this regard, Sapphira's story is a cautionary tale warning of the folly associated with possessive love. Wade is no more successful at owning Sapphira than Ruby is at controlling the philandering Junior Lee. As the islanders are quick to point out, Sapphira is, in truth, "nobody's slave" (80).

Among Willow Springs residents ritual practices such as conjure, midwifery, folk healing, and quilting bridge the gulf between house and field, village and bush, private and public in ways that signal an expanded sphere of influence on the part of Sapphira and her descendants. Ultimately, then, the ambiguity surrounding the island matriarch's life serves as a locus for the critique of white supremacist ideology and the hierarchal roles such a philosophy inscribes. George tells Cocoa as they visit the Wade estate, "A slave hadn't lived in this house. And without a slave, there could be no master" (225). Allegations of Sapphira's alleged conjuring of Wade, or her purported murder of him, raise critical questions regarding the coerced submission to the sexual authority represented by the slave master.[10] What prompts him to deed land to her? How many of her seven sons does Wade father? Is she motivated by hate, love, or possibly both impulses? How does Sapphira manage to murder Wade with impunity? Sapphira takes her freedom in 1823, one year after Denmark Vesey's slave revolt, as if to underscore the unacknowledged role of women in black insurgence. Unlike the rebellion that Queen Nanny, leader of Jamaican maroons, inspires, or the famous Stono revolt among South Carolina slaves, however, the uprising on Sapphira's part is solitary.[11] Her acts of aggression are consistent with those attributed to black women in the African Diaspora in that those gestures are covert, isolated, and individualized rather than large-scale or collective (Aptheker; Davis, *Women, Race;* Fox-Genovese). Rejecting the practice of infanticide, a revolutionary gesture targeted toward the slaveholding aristocracy, she births, names, and mothers her seven sons. Sapphira's actions lend credence to assertions that black women were not passive in the face of slaveholding aristocracy but actively opposed the white oppressor. Nat Turner faces hanging, a fate often befalling black insurrectionists, yet like the wily trickster, Sapphira escapes the hangman's noose, "laughing in a burst of flames" (3).

Distinct from Chesnutt, whose clever ex-slave narrator is singularly triumphant against a white northern businessman and the capitalist system of a southern nobility, Naylor conflates antecedent sources in rewriting the story of Sapphira, lending a new twist to an old saga involving master-slave liaisons, even as she genders the subject female, intricate, and self-determining in the face of hegemonic authority. With its dual directions conveyed largely through nuances of meaning associated with the veiled reference to crossing over, the narrative leads away from the tension embodied in the conflicted Day family past and toward a futuristic realm where hierarchal raced, gendered distinctions no longer exist. Mama Day locates the aging bill of sale at the other place. The words of the legal document attesting to Wade's purchase of Sapphira have faded, and the only words left are "Law. Knowledge. Witness. Inflicted. Nurse. Conditions. Tender. Kind" (280). Lindsey Tucker asserts that the inability to decode the writing represents "the islanders' refusal to be governed by the discourses of the oppressor."[12] Helene Christol's reading of the meaning underlying the words on the fading bill of sale goes a step further than that of Tucker when highlighting the symbolic significance of the document in terms of the way Naylor constitutes home and the self within a revolutionary domestic space where the code of male dominance loses all relevance: "The words of the message emphasize the new code (law reinforced by knowledge) whose key words are 'tender' and 'kind.'"[13] In the end, the terms scripted on the aging document herald the creation of a world order that is at once old yet characteristically new and bound with a radically transformed domestic arena.

Neither George nor Cocoa is, at first, capable of crossing over to the realm where each abandons the myths inscribed in a colonialist ideology and embraces a home reconstituted only through cultural memory and accessible by way of the vernacular. The harder he and Cocoa try to disengage themselves from the Wade-Sapphira yarn, the more they, like Br'er Rabbit fixed on the Tar-Baby, reveal their entrapment within the discourses of the dominant culture. While visiting the antebellum Wade estate, symbol for aristocratic masculine authority, George and Cocoa discuss the possibility of taking up residence in Willow Springs. Cocoa offers a sarcastic response to George's suggestion that he can succeed at the agricultural lifestyle valued among islanders: "Okay, George. This is what you want to hear: anywhere in the world you go and anything you want to do, I'm game. I'll freeze myself, starve myself, wear Salvation Army clothes to be by your side. I'll steal for you, lie for you, crawl on my hand and knees beside you. Because a good woman always follows her man" (221). Cocoa, of course, has no intention of playing the subservient role invoked in her rendering of a plantation myth concerning the southern belle. The irony underlying George's wry comment about playing Adam and Eve is not lost on the reader, or on Susan Meisenhelder, for that matter, who acknowledges the seditious role Eve plays in the Genesis myth.[14] Both Cocoa and George are enmeshed in a tangled web of competing myths concerning the gender positions that hinder the couple from enjoying a harmonious married life.

Being around Living Mirrors

In fictionalizing the legend of Sapphira, Naylor mediates between a range of texts as she seeks to create an interstitial reality where individuals are allowed to realize their unlimited identity and potential. Unlike *Linden Hills,* with its account of Willa the beleaguered housewife whose discovery of the documents that her maternal forebears author culminates in death, narrative action in *Mama Day* leads to an idealized home that refigures not only the centuries-old patriarchal Nedeed mansion in Naylor's second novel but also the nineteenth-century Wade-Sapphira estate with its history of domestic strife. Mama Day's identity as New World trickster underscores the place of the vernacular in the recovery of this space. As the mediating transatlantic figure uniting black cultures across the African Diaspora and a guardian of crossroads and entrances, Mama Day embodies a reconciliation of the dialectical tension between masculine and feminine, self and other, sacred and profane. She fulfills the role that Henry Louis Gates Jr. ascribes to Esu-Elegbara, divine trickster of Yoruba mythology, offering individuals in transit a pathway leading through oral expression (6). Although Susan Meisenhelder asserts that the world view in *Mama Day* is not tragic, her reading of George as someone whose ignorance of and disdain for the feminine results in "his recapitulating the tragic love stories of Bascombe Wade and John-Paul" fails to take into account the complexity of Mama Day's logic in sending George to the chicken coop.[15] Daphne Lamothe offers a more accurate assessment of George's perilous rite of passage when she suggests that Mama Day's words stem from an awareness of the ways that the gendered difference that George embodies is "just as vital as her own strength and resources to the salvation of her niece."[16] Indeed, the veiled words that the daughter of Legba proffers are as much a test of George's willingness to cross over—that is, enter into a realm where one is able to mediate between aspects of difference—as much as they are a coded map leading away from the danger associated with Western rational thought. She therefore offers the cryptic advice George is to follow if he is to ensure Cocoa's recovery: "There are two ways anybody can go when they come to certain roads in life," she tells George. " . . . [A]in't about a right way or a wrong way—just two ways. And here we getting down to my way or yours. Now, I got a way for us to help Baby Girl. And I'm hoping it's the one you'll use" (295). Naylor points out that George is to join hands with Mama Day in a symbolic display of communal solidarity rather than depend own his own ability in rebuilding the bridge destroyed during the storm.[17] Because the literal-minded engineer is either unable or unwilling to follow Mama Day's cryptic instructions, death is the penalty exacted for the outsider's failure to decipher the trickster's lore. Ironically, as if to underscore the enriching duality often associated with the trickster's words, George's journey leads to Mama Day's desired goal: a return on the part of both George and Cocoa to a place that is neither linguistically coded nor geographically marked.

The fact that Mama Day is unable (or perhaps unwilling) to locate a picture of George is consistent with Naylor's emphasis on the unreliability of artificial attempts to mark blackness. George is not to be *imaged,* an inadequate medium for recording the black subject, but re-*imagined,* in mnemonic fashion, in dynamic re-creation of a hybrid self not enclosed by national boundaries. Cocoa's declaration that her son "was named after a man who looked just like love" (310) recalls both the meaning Naylor ascribes to "the other place" as another narrative plane where love and magic prevail[18] and the terms inscribed on the fading bill of sale: "love," "tender," and "kind" (280). After undergoing her crucible, Cocoa finds peace in the middle with Mama Day as a guide along a path leading to a New World Order of domestic harmony—a metaphysical site recalling both Naylor's remembrance of her grandmother's "down-home" Harlem residence and the middle passage—where dialectical tensions cease.

That Mama Day uncovers the century-old well where Peace dies is a symbolic act paving the way for an end to the conflicted

Day family history involving masculine efforts to curtail female autonomy. As one who is gifted with second sight, she realizes that Cocoa is as much a victim of what Franz Fanon describes as the neurosis associated with life in a colonized setting as she is a casualty of Ruby's malevolent magic (83–108). Cocoa, who is healed within the context of Abigail's bedroom and bath, a utopian home place that reifies the female ancestor and ancient curative rituals, becomes the child that Mama Day never bore. Mama Day assumes the role of Grace, Cocoa's deceased mother in a global association of women across the African Diaspora.

Cocoa's journey toward wholeness is illuminated through the role ascribed to mirrors. At first, she gazes into a mirror and is repelled by her disheveled appearance. Later, when she looks into the mirror—one bearing a diagonal crack that is the result of a display of anger during childhood—she sees a reflection of an intact, healthy body. But she is not physically intact. In order for her to be healed she must acknowledge the reality of her malady. In other words, Cocoa has to question the authority of the fractured mirror if she is to realize the complex self that the "living mirrors" figured by a transnational maternal household image (48). Her gradual mistrust of the mirror as an accurate reflection of the self constitutes a turning point in her recovery, when she comes to rely solely upon the spiritual vision, or, more accurately, third sight, that empowers Mama Day: "So the mirror was never to be trusted. Trust only your natural eyesight. Only what you literally see is real" (281). In a representative gesture rife with folkloric significance, Abigail covers all the mirrors in the house.

At the novel's end, the real (ailing) Cocoa becomes a fiction and the imaged (healed) Cocoa becomes a reality in a fusion of the split between self and other, subject and object. Both Cocoa and George have, at last, crossed over to a place where identity is not restricted by imposed boundaries. Cocoa therefore emerges from the recesses of domestic space as a hybrid, speaking subject ready to (re)join the realm of language and adult experience in a participation in the myth making surrounding not only the legend but also legacy of Sapphira Wade. As if to signal her liberation from the binary thinking that befalls Reema's son, a remarried Cocoa resides midway between urban New York and rural Willow Springs in Charleston, a neo–briar patch, where she is free from forced limits. She neither recapitulates to the romanticized African past that lures Sapphira nor aligns herself with the institutions of mainland society. Cocoa defines herself on her own terms, and by doing so she signals her skillfulness in navigating the broad-based landscape of contemporary social relations.

The revelation that a forthcoming novel will entail a continuation of Sapphira's story presents even more potential in an investigation of the dialectics of home and resistance in Naylor's expanding canon (see the interview with Naylor in the appendix). Her authorial plan entails embedding a counternarrative resonant with trickster lore involving gendered black resistance in the African Diaspora. *Mama Day* thus disrupts colonial beliefs rooted in notions of white patriarchal dominance and works to create another narrative space—a liminal home—where a new subject and text can materialize. The legend of Sapphira paves the way for infinite discursive possibility, thereby coaxing the reader to cross over, in ways that Reema's son does not, so that we might escape the Gordian knot of the trickster's riddle and recover an authentic place of openness and autonomy.

4

Mapping the New World Order:
Bailey's Café

In Search of Eve's Garden

Last in a tetralogy, *Bailey's Café* foregrounds the subversive gestures that are to empower mid-twentieth-century African Americans in the quest for wholeness, freedom, and self-identity. What is new to Naylor's evolving canon is a focus on the universal dimensions of oppression and the necessity of mounting a strategy of resistance that globalizes the struggle for positive sociopolitical change. Such a strategy involves the construction of a unifying myth that challenges colonialist inscriptions of nationhood and places of origin. In order to locate a narrative of beginnings that can offer a buffer against the larger society and its repressive ideologies, one need look no further than the collective memories of a global community of outcasts. Naylor thus assembles a transnational group of storytellers spinning tales of trauma, displacement, and maternal loss that point to the existence of a black goddess whose healing, redemptive presence joins individuals across time and space as one collective body.

The novel's vernacular roots in black music and oral lore offer a clue to understanding figurations of a prototypical maternal figure and her close association with a radically transformed domestic space. Reminiscent of the prefatory map at the beginning of *Mama Day*, the cryptic epigraph in *Bailey's Café* charts the trajectory leading to the unscripted space serving as a habitation for this elusive figure:

hush now can you hear it can't be far away

needing the blues to get there

look and you can hear it

look and you can hear

the blues open

a place never

closing: Bailey's Café.[1]

The epigraph is an interstitial text—one that harks back to the novel's antecedent beginnings in oral tradition and anticipates the discrete linguistic patterns in the narrative proper. The ambiguous admonition to look and thus hear recalls a similar urging in *Mama Day* where the communal narrator encourages the reader-audience to "really listen" in a reification of intuitive thinking or the alternate ways of knowing. One must abandon essentialist thought before entering the intensely feminine world that Naylor constructs—a liminal space where the meaning associated with an established linguistic order loses all validity.

In this regard, Bailey's Café, way station for a multinational group of citizens in transit, and Eve's place, domicile for a largely female assembly, serve as institutional sites positioned along a path leading to freedom from imposed limits. It is Bailey, the fatherly war veteran and café proprietor, who gives a clue to the vernacular and its role in allowing access to the places through which Naylor's fictional characters must pass in the journey toward self-identity. He informs the reader, "Anything really worth hearing in this greasy spoon happens under the surface. You need to know that if you plan to stick around here and listen while we play it all out" (35). Naylor's revisionist strategy prompts a reconfiguration of geographic boundaries demarcating the magically real café. In *Mama Day,* George Andrews claims that he is able to see the restaurant when he is in New York. In *Bailey's Café,* however, the author undermines George's rationalist perspective and that of the reader when pointing out that " . . . the place sits right on the margin between the edge of the world and infinite possibility . . ." (76). Later the omniscient narrator reveals that "one can find Bailey's Café in any town" (112).

The path mapping the journey to the café leads through the vernacular and reveals the presence of fluid, increasingly expanding boundaries that allow access to a blueslike space of dynamic potentiality. Figured by the dark expanse behind the restaurant, itself situated at the liminal crossroads, this place can yield either hope or despair. It is in a site of intermediacy that the characters encounter Eve, the culmination of a long line of central mother figures in Naylor's canon and the woman who best represents the enriching complexity associated with black maternity. "Mood Indigo," Sadie's narrative of her frustrating search for belonging in the urban Midwest, underscores the collective need for the sense of stability that a connection with maternal origins can bring. The desire for belonging propels Sadie forward in life as she attempts to find the unconditional love and acceptance she does not receive from her mother, a free-spirited, abusive woman intent on immersing herself and her only child in a lifestyle of drinking and prostitution. That Sadie acquires the name "The One the Coat Hanger Missed," a constant reminder of the botched operation that her mother undergoes in a failed attempt at abortion, suggests the deep-seated nature of the rejection she experiences early in life. Little is known of Sadie's father aside from his immersion in the reckless behavior to which the mother is given. Naylor reveals that he uses the excuse of going out to buy a carton of milk as a pretense to abandon his family. The absence of detailed information about Sadie's father places the responsibility for Sadie's plight with the young woman's mother. Sadie's attempts at being a model child reflect the female socialization that she experiences, and she willingly adopts the docile, accommodating demeanor expected of young women.

An adherence to a socially prescribed identity begins early in Sadie's life and serves as the means by which she is to earn the unconditional love and acceptance her mother withholds. As a young girl, Sadie hones the domestic pursuits that she is to carry out throughout adulthood. What is apparent from her devotion to housekeeping tasks is that Sadie has no self apart from the one the larger society confers. The chores that she performs bind her to the home in ways signaling her entrapment within a gender-specific identity. Once her mother dies, Sadie is displaced, forced to fend for herself without familial or institutional aid. That she is compelled to work as a maid for wealthy whites and, later, enter a life of prostitution is a commentary on the lack of viable options for black women in the city. Not only that, but Sadie's means of self-support sets up the dialectical tension embodied in the dichotomous roles of virgin and whore that, according to Naylor, delimit women's achievement and identity.[2] By selling her body, Sadie positions herself outside the pale of the prim, proper, ladylike posture she sought to maintain.

But Naylor endows Sadie with a complexity that encourages the reader to rethink constructions of female sexuality present in the larger society. Even though the woman is a prostitute, it is out of an effort to survive that she sells her body, and she is careful to charge only what she needs in order to pay her bills. Naylor paints Sadie using broad strokes so that the woman defies the stereotypic image of the hypersexual black female. Throughout Sadie's narrative she persists in her efforts to transform the miscellaneous dwellings she is forced to inhabit into the place she associates with home. While she is thirteen years old, she envisions an idealized homestead complete with a picket fence and lush garden: "There was to be a trim white bungalow with a green picket fence, and she would keep the front yard swept clean of leaves and pick all the withered blooms from their fence full of roses" (44). Sadie's dream-fantasy home evolves out of her rich interior life. For this daughter of displaced southern migrants, home assumes archetypal dimensions and is bound with an agrarian ideal reminiscent of her parents' rural past—a place far removed from the squalor and decadence of Chicago's South Side. It is the dream and its promise of familial stability that both sustains and eludes Sadie in her search for a place of fulfillment and belonging.

Marriage to Daniel, an abusive alcoholic who is thirty years Sadie's senior, frustrates her efforts to realize the home she envisions. Not only does Daniel exert tyrannical control over his passive wife, but he does so in ways that resemble the abuse Sadie endures in her relationship with her mother: "She went off with a man older than enough to be her father, and she ended up living with her mother again for the next twenty-five years" (51). Sadie is immersed in a seemingly endless round of cooking and cleaning, with Daniel's three-room shanty as a site for the woman's performance of the housekeeping tasks that prevent her from realizing her potential. The only respite from her monotonous routine occurs when she is in her garden, a gendered space of female creativity linking the troubled woman with countless other black women.

Daniel's death frees Sadie from the strictures of domesticity and thrusts her outward into a male-dominated marketplace in search of employment. Drawing upon the domestic skills she acquires early in life, she turns to day work in an effort to earn the money needed to purchase the house she once shared with Daniel. A chance encounter with a white prostitute who once employed Sadie underscores the desperate situation of black women in the city. While the former madam is married and living in a mansion with a college-bound daughter, Sadie is an aging, single woman limited to menial jobs with low wages and dismal working conditions. That she eventually loses the home she tries so hard to keep and is forced to move to a tenement and, later, a woman's shelter is a reminder of persistent homelessness that the woman tries in vain to escape. Ultimately, Sadie is forced onto the streets as she joins the ranks of countless other displaced city residents, with her five-star wine and prostitution as her only means of survival.

Sadie's courtship with Iceman Jones, a kindly widower whose tragic story rivals hers, serves to revive memories of the woman's idealized home. Recounted from her point of view, the couple's courtship underscores Sadie's continuing desire for a place of belonging:

> Sadie allowed Iceman Jones to come as far as the picket
> fence that night. Under the stars she stood with her hand
> discreetly on the gate latch so he'd understand this was where
> she wanted to visit. There was a gentle wind that fluttered the
> voile curtains in the lighted kitchen window and brought the
> aroma of her chicken casserole. It was still too early in spring
> for the geraniums to be blooming, but she pointed out the
> mulched beds that would soon bear her Martha Washingtons
> and trailers. She'd thought about roses, she told him, but be-
> lieve it or not, even the American Beauties don't get as red as
> these, and roses are finicky, they wouldn't hold up with the
> trains. (72)

Sadie's dream-fantasy courtship takes place within the framework
of a setting that is at once both urban and rural; past, present, and
future coalesce in the woman's vision involving Iceman Jones's visit.
What she conceives of are the possibilities for a harmonious married life, even in the midst of a hostile city environment.

Jones represents a last opportunity to reverse the cycle of displacement defining her existence. As if to indicate the woman's willingness to entertain the promise associated with marriage, Sadie's
imaginary courtship continues with a rendering of a down-home
dinner. She allows Jones to be seated on her front porch, and later,
as the two dine on chicken casserole, she is careful to use her Water-
ford crystal. In order to maintain the appearance of propriety, however, Sadie keeps the home well lit: "The first time the man's in your
home, you don't want him thinking you're forward. No, her good
china, her good glasses, and a very simple meal: baked chicken,
spinach, boiled potatoes, and a store-bought cake for dessert. She
knew men—start too soon with homemade cakes and they start
getting nervous" (75).

It is indeed disappointing that the aging widow refuses Iceman
Jones's proposal, a decision that likely means she will never escape
the stranglehold of Chicago's South Side. Jones's mistake is in offer-

ing a life lived on his terms, not hers: "She knew this dear man was offering her the moon, but she could give him the stars" (78). Narrative emphasis on "moon" and "stars" refers ambiguously to both the tension between masculine and feminine largely responsible for Sadie's entrapment within a gender-specific role and the five-star wine the woman drinks. At her story's end, Sadie wanders eternally in the dark expanse located behind the café, ever in search of a communal space of unconditional acceptance. Dorothy Thompson's reading of the novel leads her to conclude that "Sadie's liminal state—she is caught between her daydreams of being a fine lady and her actual existence as wino/whore—leaves her short of the aggregation that Eve's brownstone offers: a (comm)unity of sisters (same profession) who have the advantage of ritual (rules and tradition) and a cultural mother-necromancer."[3] Sadie's failure to find Eve's residence places the woman outside the perimeters of the restorative bond uniting the female boarders in their association with a transcendent mother figure.

Myths of a semidivine maternal character find fullest expression in the exploits on the part of Eve, an ambiguous persona who hails from the Delta region of Louisiana, as if to convey her close affinity with African creole traditions involving magic, mysticism, and the supernatural. "Eve's Song," with its rendering of her move toward autonomy and self-definition, evolves out of the nexus between oral and written lore surrounding the exploits of extraordinary women who achieve renown for their tendency to usurp male authority. Her intense spirituality, along with her ability to embody both masculine and feminine, invite a comparison with the qualities characterizing an assortment of African queens and goddesses. In his examination of ancient matriarchal patterns, Ivan Van Sertima seeks to explore the scholarship surrounding an African Eve originating in Ethiopia (*Black Women in Antiquity*). Much like *Mama Day*'s Sapphira Wade, Eve exhibits traits Teresa Washington would ascribe to aje; Naylor's central mother figure is ageless, timeless, and genderless (*Our Mothers, Our Powers, Our Texts*). She is the first customer to arrive at the café, and her thousand-year trek from Pilottown to New Orleans is one that confirms her preeminence among a transnational community of outcasts.

Eve's exalted role as healer, midwife, and guide points to the existence of a revitalized social order involving a reification of the feminine and its association with unrestrained creativity. Naylor refigures the patriarchal story of Adam and Eve in Genesis through the presentation of a self-determining female character whose very existence calls into question masculine privilege and rule. The fictional Eve therefore defines herself in opposition to Godfather, the stern, dictatorial preacher who rears her. The institutional control that Godfather exerts is evident by his influence within the realms of knowledge, religion, and commercial enterprise. "The town had only three buildings that qualified as such: the school, the cotton exchange, and the church," Eve tells the reader regarding life in Pilottown. "He was the preacher in one, the scale foreman and bookkeeper in the another, and no one attended the drafty school past the ninth grade" (85). The revelation of the circumstances surrounding Eve's birth suggests that she owes no allegiance to any masculine entity, human or divine. "Godfather always said that he made me," she relates, "but I was born of the delta" (90). As if in opposition to the biblical story of Eve's development from Adam's rib, Naylor constructs an alternate account of beginnings that encourages an association between the fictional Eve and the rich Louisiana soil. Eve's burgeoning sexuality, given fullest expression during earth stomping with the childish prankster Billy Boy, suggests the oneness that the novel's central mother figure shares with the earth.

Godfather's banishment of Eve sets the stage for the autonomous, self-determining life that she leads. Once Eve is thrust out of Pilottown, she is forced to fend for herself without the benefit of familial or institutional support. Her ten-year stint in New Orleans allows her to acquire three steamer trunks of imported suits, thousands of dollars, and a keen affection for gardens (91). Eve is the quintessential self-made woman whose thousand-year trek to Bailey's Café signals her evolution from a position where she is subject to masculine authority to a place where she sets the terms of her own existence. A radical restructuring of society's identity politics occurs as Eve arrives at the café: "I had no choice but to walk into New Orleans neither male nor female—mud. But I could right then and there choose what I was going to be when I walked back out" (91).

The metamorphosis that Eve undergoes during her journey earns her the position she assumes as proprietor of the boardinghouse/bordello offering sanctuary to a largely female group, and like Papa Legba of African folklore fame, she serves as medium and guide to a host of weary travelers in search of a place of refuge. Her home is a feminine place of healing, renewal, and rebirth recalling similar textual spaces in the tradition of women's writing. Lily, the white female protagonist in Sue Monk Kidd's novel *The Secret Life of Bees*, fulfills her need for a divine female archetype within the spiritual practices of a group of southern African American sisters. And bell hooks describes her grandmother's rural Kentucky residence as a feminine site of caring and sustenance:

> In our young minds houses belonged to women, were their special domain, not as property, but as places where all that truly mattered in life took place—the warmth and comfort of shelter, the feeding of our bodies, the nurturing of our souls. There we learned dignity, integrity of being; there we learned to have faith. The folks who made this life possible, who were our primary guides and teachers, were black women. (42)

Eve's actions might seem bizarre, even malevolent at times, in ways that place her at odds with the idealized maternal figure hooks recalls, but she remains as an archetypal figure at the center of the reconstituted multinational household Naylor constructs. With Esther, whose sense of self-worth is undermined because of subjectivity to patriarchal privilege, Eve allows the young woman to regain the dignity she forfeits as a consequence of the commodity status ascribed to the black female within a capitalist system. Esther is relegated to being a concubine, and her story is situated within the larger historic framework of slavery and share farming as her brother barters her in exchange for higher wages. The older farmer who purchases Esther assumes a dual role as husband and master, subjecting the young woman to acts of sadomasochism in a darkened cellar. Signaling the ways in which women often act as agents of female oppression, the farmer's wife bathes Esther in preparation for the sexual abuse that the young woman endures.

The interior monologues appearing throughout Esther's story reveal the extent to which the young woman has internalized the negative self-image that the larger society assigns. Esther not only lacks a positive sense of self, but her private recollections indicate that she lives in a world that evolves no terms for her existence: "I like the white roses because they show up in the dark. I don't. The black gal. Monkey face. Tar. Coal. Soot. Unspeakable. Pitch. Coal. Ugly. Soot. Unspeakable" (95). It is significant, however, that she tells her own story, thereby exercising a level of authorial control over the circumstances that have delineated her existence. Residency at Eve's place offers a starting point for the young woman's recovery. That she demands white roses from her gentleman callers and is to be called "Little Sister" suggests a reaffirmation of Esther's virtue. She therefore lends her solitary voice to those of the other narrators whose stories comprise "The Jam."

The role that Eve plays as healer is especially evident in the dramatic recovery that Jesse Bell undergoes. Jesse is a spirited, outspoken woman whose efforts to find fulfillment by marrying into the wealthy Sugar Hill King family fail when she meets with rejection from her snobbish father-in-law. Uncle Eli's disdain for the down-home rituals and traditions of the working-class Bell family prompts him to humiliate Jesse at every turn, even to the point where he turns her own son against her. Perhaps if her husband had been willing to stand alongside her after news of her lesbianism becomes public, the couple's marriage might have lasted or, at the very least, Jesse could have held onto some semblance of dignity in light of her arrest. But the woman is left to deal with her situation on her own.

Jesse crosses class lines in her marriage into the King family. Much of her narrative involves the contrast between the aristocratic lifestyle of Sugar Hill residents and the down-home rituals and traditions of the Bell family. Jesse is from a long line of strong women, and she undergoes a dramatic shift in her status once she moves into the elitist neighborhood. Among wealthy Sugar Hill residents, women are expected to subordinate their aspirations in ways that enhance a patriarchal social arrangement. Jesse soon learns that the wives are often subject to domestic violence. Her description of her tumultuous nineteen-year marriage is steeped in terms suggestive of her dynamic subjectivity as she moves from one social group to the next:

> ... [N]obody was interested in my side of the story, not the reporters, not the neighbors, not the divorce court, nobody, cause everybody was standing around like vultures looking at me fall fall fall, waiting for me to smash my brains on the pavement, yeah, waiting for me to lose my mind; and within a inch of the ground, within a inch of having my head split open and my brains spill out, Jesse Bell grabbed onto the reins of that white horse, letting 'em all see her spread wings as she rose. (131–32)

Emphasis on ascent and descent underscores Jesse's changing subject position as she moves from a familial space in which women enjoy a measure of autonomy to a setting where the middle-class wife is forced to surrender her self-identity. Such an emphasis also directs attention to the heroin she turns to as a way of coping with her marital problems.

As in *Linden Hills,* Naylor uses marriage as a locus for the critique of bourgeoisie ideology and patriarchal ideas concerning woman's place. The birth of Jesse's son serves to enhance the King family's paternal lineage in a situation where the middle-class wife and mother has no self apart from the social role she assumes. But like the Nedeed wives, who found inventive ways of countering the imposition of patriarchal rule, Jesse manages to exercise agency in her dealings with the masculinist system responsible for the oppression she faces. The distressed wife finds solace in the arms of her female lover in ways that herald Jesse's eventual move to Eve's boardinghouse/bordello, a space allowing her to achieve a communal bond with women who are similarly displaced from home and family. It is significant in an understanding of her evolutionary growth that she tells her own story, thereby challenging the perspective of Bailey, who sets up her narrative and, equally as important, the point of view of the local newspaper with its lurid account of her arrest and divorce. Jesse informs the reader, "And I was a good wife. I mean, a good wife. But I didn't have no friends putting out the *Herald Tribune*. And it's all about who's in charge of the keeping of the records, ain't it?" (118). As the woman who proudly announces, "I got the reputation for being a real nasty bitch," she tells her story in order to clarify her true motives (124).

Naylor's revision of the story of the biblical Jezebel, whose name is bound with ideas of transgressive female sexuality, reveals Jesse's efforts to be a model wife. By no means is Jesse the "nasty bitch" others regard her as. It is because of the interference from Uncle Eli that she is compelled to define herself in ways that bourgeois society deems unacceptable. Jesse is a woman who is intent on pleasing her man. Cooking offers a direct link between the Bell family's working-class lifestyle and the upper-middle-class Sugar Hill community. Jesse relies upon her feminine charms as much as her culinary skills:

> The next night I baked three sweet-potato pies. I mean, the heavy kind with lard in the crust and Alaga syrup bubbling all through them. And while my pies are cooling and he's in the

bedroom reading his newspaper, I run me a warm bath and throw a whole bottle of vanilla extract in the water. So I'm soaking in the vanilla, the pies are cooling, and we're all ready about the same time. I go into our bedroom, carrying one of my pies, dressed the same way I stepped out of the tub. (124)

Jesse's bold display of sensuality fails to safeguard her marriage from the machinations of her meddling father in law. Only in the context of the communal household represented by Eve's boardinghouse/ bordello does the troubled woman find the unconditional acceptance central to her restoration.

That Jesse achieves recognition among a congregation of women is a result of Eve's interventionist role in reversing the psychological distress that has prompted Jesse's drug addiction. The novel's central mother figure intercedes only after the troubled woman reaches the lowest point in life. As part of Eve's unconventional therapy, Jesse is forced to gaze into the void behind the café, a space that can yield either hopelessness or endless possibility. Eve conjures a scene evolving out of the women's shared pasts involving a vision of a bedroom and bath. Complete with a raw pine floor, chenille spread, and rosewood rocker, the imagined domestic space stands in stark contrast with the homes the women have fled. So vivid is the dream-fantasy home that Jesse is able to hear her mother wrestling with an old wooden kitchen stove and smell fried fish and turnip greens. Dorothy Thompson's reading of the novel suggests that the "symbols in the scene add up to an indictment of the Western images and ideals that destroy little black girls who cannot mirror and attain them."[4] While the experiences of Eve and Jesse Bell underscore the debilitating effects of the larger society and its definitions of femininity, the domestic space that the women see serves to divest them of the cultural myths the larger society perpetuates. In other words, Eve must first reify the false images that are responsible for the women's loss of self before Jesse can find the self-identity existing only within the context of an idealized domestic space that is at once both cultured and gendered.

Eve bathes the distressed Jesse Bell in a ritual of healing reminiscent of Mattie's bathing of the bereaved Lucielia Louise Turner in *The Women of Brewster Place* and Miranda's bathing of the bewitched Cocoa in *Mama Day*. Here, in Naylor's fourth text, there is direct association between the maternal figure as a redemptive agent and her semidivine female counterpart in ancient lore. Jesse becomes the child of Eve, mother of all living, while Eve assumes the role of Jesse's mother in a symbolic re-creation of the mother-daughter relationship. As part of her rather unconventional cure of the drug-addicted Jesse Bell, Eve allows her to have unlimited access to heroin. Jesse may question Eve's unorthodox methods, but the novel's central mother accomplishes what scores of rehabilitation centers have been unable to do: Jesse, the reader learns, is cured in less than a month.

The repartee between Eve and Sister Carrie underscores the significance of Eve's boardinghouse/bordello as ritual grounds for the transformation that displaced women undergo. When Sister Carrie uses the Bible to condemn Jesse Bell's lesbianism, Eve, who is reared by a preacher, relies upon Scripture as well: "Thou also, which hast judged thy sisters, bear thy shame for thy sins that thou has committed more abominable than they: they are more righteous than thou: yea, be thou confounded also and bear thy shame, in that thou has justified thy sisters" (135). In her citation of this Old Testament passage from Ezekiel, Eve signals the presence of a transcendent sisterhood between women across time and space. Notions of sexual difference that have resulted in the circumscription of the female self come under scrutiny in her spirited response. Eve undermines Sister Carrie's homophobic perspective and encourages a democratic stance toward issues of morality set forth in divine law.

Rewriting the Virgin-Whore Dichotomy:
A Tale of Two Marys

In rewriting the antecedent sources out of which *Bailey's Café* evolves, Naylor seeks to dismantle the negative images that delimit female identity and achievement. Issues relevant to female sexuality assume center stage with the antithetical representations of virgin and whore. "Mary: Take Two," a reworking of the Virgin Birth, is based upon the Mariology of Judeo-Christian biblical history. The use of the name Mary with regard to both the sexually alluring Peaches and the Ethiopian-born virgin Mariam, whose name is a Hebrew variation of Mary, raises important questions regarding proscriptions of women's sexuality. In *The Virgin Mary in the Perceptions of Women,* Joelle Mellon traces the contradictory images of passive virgin and repentant whore throughout pre-Christian and Christian history. A juxtaposition of the two fictional characters and their unique histories serves a fertile site for an examination of the universal dimensions of oppression and efforts to redefine the terms of black female identity.

While Peaches's burgeoning sexuality serves as an occasion to indulge the passions of the men who view her as an object of desire, Mariam is the untouched virgin whose clitoridectomy will ensure that she remains pure until marriage. The Kansas-born Peaches is a light-skinned beauty who is "a cocoa-butter dream" (101); Mariam, a fourteen-year-old displaced citizen of Addis Ababa, is an outcast among orthodox Jews and is too dim-witted to be able to tell her own story. Despite the apparent differences between the two women, they are subjugated in a world that defines them as a passive, subservient other. For Peaches, it is the miscellaneous men intent on sexual exploitation and her well-intentioned father who set the terms for her existence. Mariam is no less entrapped than her American-born counterpart, but Naylor's rendering of the young woman's journey to Bailey's Café underscores not only the role of Scripture in perpetuating female oppression but also the ways that women serve as agents of masculine domination. Repetition of "No man has ever touched men" serves as a refrain highlighting women's complicity in patriarchal rule (143, 44, 45, 46).

Peaches's journey to Eve's place reveals the dynamics of the young woman's attempts to distance herself from the harmful, controlling images present in the larger society. The stages involved in her evolutionary move toward self-identity reveal her conscious rejection of the objectified self that her well-intentioned father and other men project. At first she tries to suppress her sexualized self. Later, escapades with men become her way of exercising autonomy apart from the restrictions of her domineering father. The mirrors that Peaches encounters chart her path toward self-identity. Envisioning herself through the false image that others ascribe to her allows her to stand back from artificial designations of the female persona in ways that signal her shift toward independence from an oppressive social order. As if to signal the new self that Peaches realizes, she refers to herself using the third person.

Peaches forms an alternate identity that exists in opposition to the one that the larger society prescribes. Much of her narrative involves her symbolic journey to the place that Cocoa arrives at after her ritual healing as a result of Mama Day's maternal influence. An act of self-mutilation signals Peaches's rejection of the image patriarchal society ascribes and her willingness to embrace the redemptive circle of female sisters at Eve's place. The young woman uses a beer can opener to cut her face, and by so doing, she disassociates herself from false self-image that has delimited her achievement:

> I walked out of the hospital free do whatever I wanted. And since he had started me on the railroads going east, I kept going east. It gave me pleasure to sit on the right side of the train aisle to watch through the window's reflection as one of them moved hopefully toward the empty seat beside me. I'd show off my good left dimple when he asked if the seat was free. Yes, I'd answer, and so am I. (111)

Eve's declaration to Peaches's father, "Go home, my friend. I'll return your daughter to you whole," reveals the transformation the young woman is to undergo (114). As if to signal her new social identity among a community of women, not only is Peaches present among the multinational group gathered at George's birth, but she is first to intone the gospel song that inscribes the child's sacred identity.

Writing the Black Man's Blues

Naylor's fourth novel foregrounds the transnational journey home in ways that encourage the reader to rethink predictable ways of knowing and adopt a new basis for self and society—one predicated upon the feminine. In this regard, Eve's place serves as a liminal space of becoming and possibility recalling the middle passage and the cross-cultural exchange leading to the creation of a dynamic identity. The presence of Miss Maple among an otherwise exclusively female household raises questions about the feminine and its implications for masculinity. What unites him with the female narrators is his entrapment within socially prescribed gender roles. That his story is situated against a backdrop involving tension between Mexico, Texas, and California serves to locate his quest for self-identity within the context of the border strife in the American Southwest. Miss Maple is a border subject whose heritage includes American Indian, European, Mexican, African, and Spanish ancestry. Despite the fact of his multicultural identity, he is subject to the larger society's tendency toward reductive racial categorization.

Miss Maple's father, a refined, erudite man with a love for the classics, offers an image of maleness that is at once both enabling and contradictory. The father's insistence upon a definition of manhood existing apart from the exercise of sexual prowess places the son in a position where he questions his own masculinity. In response to the images of maleness represented in Shakespeare's plays, Miss Maple announces, "Manhood is a pervasive preoccupation when you're an adolescent boy, and you tend to see a fairy under every bush" (175). Miss Maple is a transgendered character who prefigures the cross-dressing Chino in *The Men of Brewster Place*. Unlike the flamboyant, sadomasochistic Chino, Miss Maple is not gay; the one encounter Miss Maple has with a male occurs in prison and takes place when he is coerced into submission. Naylor's description of the sole male resident at Eve's place as "the manliest man she has ever known" reveals her attempt to expand her efforts at dismantling society's identity politics so that she challenges socially constructed notions of masculinity.[5]

If Miss Maple's father is a catalyst for the son's sexual anxiety, he is also the medium for the dynamic self-reflection that prompts Miss Maple to distance himself from the ideas of machismo that govern social relations in America's southwestern border region. An encounter with the Gatlins, a gang of poor, ignorant vigilante whites, is the defining moment for the father and son. The Gatlins urinate on the father's books and lock the father-son duo in a storeroom in an expression of a disdain for the renaissance lifestyle that the father valorizes. In his attempt to escape his entrapment, Miss Maple's father dons a corset and lace crinoline as he fights his way out of his the room.

The father's cross-dressing masquerade offers an alternate model of self-identity for Miss Maple, whose decision to adopt modes of dress from a range of cultures reflects his adoption of a fluid persona existing in opposition to the essentialist self that the Gatlins impose. Much of his narrative involves his frustrating efforts to find acceptance within the academy and corporate America. His refusal to define himself solely in terms of a phallocentric ideal is evident by his role as both housekeeper and bouncer at Eve's place. It is within the recesses of a female domestic space that he combines his knowledge of statistics with his creative ability in writing award winning jingles. Miss Maple's research for Armour Company reveals a keen awareness of the needs of women. He tells the reader that "the new attitudes of American housewives made them ripe for a dishwashing detergent that would leave them feeling both married and sexy" (215).

Naylor's fourth novel thus moves toward the creation of what Homi Bhabha describes as a New World (B)Order in which predetermined boundaries cease to exist (110). The refigured social order emerging in the novel's closing scene is comprised of individuals representing a range of geographies, cultures, and philosophies— all of them converging at Bailey's Café, a medial space outside of established bounds. George's long-anticipated birth occasions a coalescence of diverse cultural traditions. Gabriel, a Russian Jew, presides in the naming ceremony. He and Bailey find common ground in their dispute over the naming ritual when they discover that both of their fathers are named George. As with the biblical Gabriel, Naylor's fictional character acts as a guide to Mariam in offering her directions to the café. Peaches intones the gospel song that inscribes George's sacred identity:

> Anybody ask you who you are?
>
> Who you are?
>
> Who you are?
>
> Anybody ask you who you are?
>
> Tell him—you're the child of God. (225)

As the other members of the group join in with the singing of this popular Christmas carol, now a cultural code among an international group of outcasts, their voices unite in a call for world harmony:

> Peace on earth, Mary rocked the cradle.
>
> Mary rocked the cradle and Mary rocked the cradle.
>
> Peace on earth, Mary rocked the cradle.
>
> Tell him—was the child of God. (226)

The diverse community assembled at George's birth signals the attainment of peace, a veiled reference to a restoration of the broken black historic continuum. George's mother assumes center stage in Naylor's revision of the Virgin Birth. Naming the Ethiopian-born young woman Mariam, a variation of Mary, links the biblical mother of Christ with her ethnic (Hebrew) roots.[6] Commenting on the revisionist strategy Naylor employs in rewriting biblical texts, Dorothy Perry Thompson notes, "As an Africana womanist, Naylor constructs her text, her (re)figurations, with recursions that pay homage to the history and expressive culture of Africa and the diaspora. Mere reflection is not a stopping place for her. As she ascends to make new models, she not only revises Western tradition, but also liberates her listener/reader."[7] Through his maternal association with the young Ethiopian Jew, George acquires an identity that is at once both new and old. His new identity, which is ritualized within a community of outcasts, challenges assertions of illegitimacy present in accounts of his mysterious parentage. In *Cult of the Black Virgin,* Ean Begg writes, "The Black Virgin is a Christian phenomenon as well as a preservation of the ancient goddesses and compensates for the one-sided conscious attitudes of the age" (131). He goes on to say, "As the spirit of light in darkness she comes to break the chains of those who live in the prison of unconsciousness and restore them to their true home. In the trackless forest she is both the underground magnetism and the intuition that senses it, pointing the traveler in the right direction. She is traditionally the compassionate one" (134). A reification of this figure in the person of Mariam thus represents a symbolic recovery of a lost past that offers a starting point for the recovery both she and George need.

The journey to Bailey's Café is ultimately a pilgrimage leading back to the rich cultural traditions of a transnational community and vernacular accounts of an archetypal black goddess with ties to ancient Africa. As a result of Naylor's efforts to highlight the experiences of a diverse group of displaced citizens of the world, the household emerging in the novel's culminating scene is global in nature and represents a range of cultures, religions, and ethnicities. That this assembly is as eclectic as it is, and is unified around the presence of Mariam and George, suggests the power and preeminence of the feminine as an enabling, creative source. George's characteristically postcolonial anxiety of origins thus finds resolution, not in the institutions of the West, figured by Wallace P. Andrews's Boys' Shelter, but in a timeless African heritage involving the acts of an exalted black female ancestor.

Conclusion

If there is a canonical story evolving out of Naylor's first four novels, that narrative involves the quest for autonomy, in both a literary and racial sense—one that is encoded in the vernacular and bound with figurations of an idealized home. For Naylor, home is a fluid space embedded in cultural memory and rooted in a past that harks back to her parents' Robinsonville, Mississippi, roots and ultimately ancient Africa. In keeping with the subversive acts on the part of an assortment of black subjects throughout the transatlantic world, Naylor's reinscription of home is a symbolic gesture of resistance directed toward the colonialist imperative responsible for the persistent condition of homelessness experienced by the border figure. Naylor rewrites home, but she does so from what I label a neo–briar patch, the unique vantage point afforded by the interplay between a multitude of diverse, often contesting positionings owing to the complexities of race, class, and gender. It is not surprising that she attributes her development as an African American woman writer to the ritual events taking place within a specifically maternal domestic space where storytelling figured as prominently as cooking and cleaning.[1] Her fictional characters often emerge from the recesses of home as speaking subjects, ready to rejoin the realm of language and adult experience. Naylor's search for an authoritative voice with which to tell or, rather, retell the stories of black women is therefore not only one that owes much of its inspiration to the everyday moments of domestic life—cooking, cleaning, sewing, and mothering—but also is paradigmatic in nature, suggesting a link or discursive bridge between her writing and that of black women across the Diaspora. Mae Gwendolyn Henderson and Carol Boyce Davies are among a growing number of scholars advocating an intellectual border crossing in dismantling boundaries between theoretical and critical writing or between the geographic borders posing an artificial distinction between black women writers in the transatlantic world.[2] Davies's observations regarding the reinscription of home on the part of the Afro-Caribbean/American creative writer are apropos in an interrogation of Naylor's fictional engagement with places of origin:

> For the writing of home exists narratively—in conversation, letters to family, telephone conversations, stories passed on to children as family history or to friends as reminiscences. Thus, the rewriting of home becomes a critical link in the articulation of identity. It is a play of resistance to domination which identifies where we come from, but also locates home in its many transgressive and disjunctive experiences. (115)

Naylor's evolving authorial voice is a multifaceted one that disrupts established inscriptions of identity and place. The largely female domestic space that she scripts in her first novel is at once both rural and urban, embedded in an agrarian history and part of a changing metropolitan landscape. Brewster Place serves as the medial space where southern migrants are allowed to redefine themselves in ways that challenge the strictures of a postwar urban bureaucracy. Through the ritual practices emanating from a pastoral setting, an otherwise fragmented community transforms its squalid environment into a nurturing site of belonging and becoming. Brewster persists long after its condemnation at the hands of the rich and powerful, and the community's expanding boundaries serve as a locus for the critique of inscribed conceptions of regional origins.

In *Linden Hills,* Naylor draws upon feminist ideology in writing back to the masculinist empire responsible for the subjugation of the Nedeed wives. Home still exists for African Americans in suburbia, but only in cultural memory, and it is bound with an agrarian ideal that is far removed from the aristocratic neighborhood. Willa is faced with the daunting task of dismantling the Nedeed Empire along with its insistence upon male domination. Even though her awakening and subsequent ascent from the basement occasion her own death as well as that of Luther, her revolutionary gesture places her in a long line of radical, proactive women who refuse to acquiesce in the face of male power. Willie, Willa's masculine counterpart, is the medium through which Naylor inscribes a gendered history of black female resistance—one that points to a destabilization of a strictly masculinist historiographic record.

If *Linden Hills* prefigures an apocalyptic end to the home under male domination, *Mama Day* offers a glimpse of an emergent social order involving a reification of the feminine. Ritual practices such as folk healing, midwifery, and conjure allow once-marginalized women to reclaim a place of prominence in everyday affairs and traverse the narrow boundaries demarcating private and public spheres. Sapphira Wade is, of course, the preeminent mother whose eternal presence serves as a guiding influence among Willow Springs' residents, and her celebrated trek back to Africa solidifies her place in community lore. But Cocoa's decision to reside in Charleston rather than in Willow Springs or New York not only complicates notions of a home tied to a romanticized Africa but also challenges ideas of a national identity tied to singularly constructed conceptions of time or space. As the descendant of both Norwegian-born Bascombe Wade and African foremother Sapphira Day, Cocoa is the quintessential border subject whose complex identity owes no loyalty to any one geographic setting.

The cornerstone of the literary foundation Naylor constructs, *Bailey's Café* examines issues of resistance and home among a multinational community of cultural orphans in search of a place of belonging. The novel's diverse assortment of storytellers gathered at Eve's boardinghouse in anticipation of George's birth allows the reader to locate the homespace in a decidedly global framework involving an erasure of national boundaries. In this regard, the Black Madonna serves as the reconciling persona uniting individuals representing a range of cultures, ethnicities, and geographies.

Because the maternal figure is central to the reinscription of home, Naylor's canon reveals an array of mothers (Eva Turner, Mattie Michael, Mamie Tilson, Roberta Johnson, Mama Day, and Eve) whose redemptive presence is crucial to the border subject's emerging self-identity. These mothers tend to be situated at the liminal crossroads between nations, between worlds, and as New World daughters of Papa Legba, they function as mediating transatlantic figures that bridge the gulf between past and present, oral and written modes of expression. If Mattie Michael signals the beginning of Naylor's fictionalization of the black mother, Eve marks the extreme limits of Naylor's reworking of the maternal, an ageless, timeless embodiment of a folk epistemology.

For Naylor, the future exists alongside the past in a careful reworking of colonialist inscriptions of time and place. Her writing reveals a concern with the social, cultural, and political issues defining a postwar landscape, and the spaces evolving out of her fiction point to a transformed social reality at odds with the tyranny of the present. Susan Willis identifies the black female author's ability to envision radically different social relationships as being the single most compelling aspect of the African American woman's novel tradition, and she rightfully asserts that the alternative future that these women project is to emerge out of the ordinary and commonplace. According to Willis,

> The future takes shape within the walls that have traditionally imprisoned women and defined their social labor: the home. Black women's writing does not explode the household nor does it situate the realization of women's potentialities in the workplace. Rather, it works on the commonplace features of daily life, from household objects to household labor, from childbearing to sexuality. It asks how these might be lifted out of the oppressive and repressive constraints defined by bourgeois society and capitalism. (159)

Commonalities between Naylor's fiction and the novels of Jamaica Kincaid, Michelle Cliff, Audre Lorde, Paule Marshall, and Nobel Prize winner Toni Morrison extend the conversation regarding home and resistance beyond a continental United States geography. Morrison's latest novel, *A Mercy,* reveals an engagement with issues of home and the struggle for autonomy during an era in which matters of identity are in their nascent stages. Florens's migratory journey from a plantation in Maryland to a New York farm assumes epic dimensions in an understanding of identity construction during the seventeenth century. The slave girl's search for the African-born blacksmith who holds the key to not only her evolving self-identity but also the healing of her mistress Rebekka is couched within the mother-daughter relationship, a nexus for examining the ambivalent, conflicted connection between the migratory subject and places of origin. The portrait of home emerging in Morrison's latest text is one comprised of blacks and Europeans, slaves and indentured servants, men and women—displaced citizens of the world faced with the task of defining and redefining the self within the in-between space of early American society. Morrison teases out issues regarding the role of re-memory and language with a rendering of life among an eclectic, largely female group of outcasts representing a range of nationalities and ethnicities. Florens has much in common with the women figuring into Naylor's canon as the displaced slave girl finds affirmation amid a congregation of marginal women. Ultimately, it is not the nameless blacksmith but Florens's guilt-stricken mother, herself an outcast and an African, who holds the key to the slave girl's journey, a literal and symbolic voyage with mnemonic overtones leading back to oral language. Naylor's writing suggests intriguing critical possibilities in an investigation of the textual spaces uniting black women novelists across the transatlantic world.

Appendix

Opening Up the Place Called Home: A Conversation with Gloria Naylor

The following interview took place between Gloria Naylor and Maxine Montgomery at Naylor's home in Brooklyn, New York, on May 3, 2007.

Maxine Montgomery: Ms. Naylor, I'd like to begin by asking you about events of national or international significance. The first has to do with the circumstances that took place on September 11, 2001. How did that event or those events affect you personally?

Gloria Naylor: Well, there was no immediate impact upon my physical environment because I live here in Brooklyn, and that was in lower Manhattan. But what I did think about with the enormity of the tragedy was the fact that this is the result of America's foreign policy. You know, America has been all over the world dumping on people, signing with leaders who are not democratic, supporting Israel in its occupational goals against the Palestinians, being totally unfair to other nations, and ultimately those actions came home to roost.

MM: Do you feel that America has changed in a lasting or meaningful way as a result of that incident?

GN: Oh definitely, definitely. Now that the terror has been brought home, Americans feel the insecurity that the rest of the world has always felt. Because terrorism is nothing new to Europe or the Middle East, Americans realize that events transpiring across the ocean have repercussions that can affect the United States. I don't know how many really realize that, Maxine, because the media is so quick to spin a story in any direction they want it to take. So they spun September 11 into a search for terrorists as opposed to a search for the reasons that these people hate us. As American citizens, we need to understand the rationale underlying the negative image that our country has in an international sphere.

MM: You speak fondly in interviews about the Black Revolution, the Civil Rights Movement, and the Million-Man March. I'm wondering if you feel as though we will ever regain the same momentum that we had in the sixties or the seventies.

GN: No. No. I don't think that is ever going to happen again, because racism has gone underground, and so you have to look for it in little, subtle ways. Since there are no more segregated bathrooms, you can't target bathrooms. The plight of blacks today is like the plight of the poor and working-class whites. Jobs have gone overseas, so there has been some mobilization against global movements like the World Trade Organization. Not long ago in Seattle, fifty thousand people showed up to protest. Because when jobs leave this country, they don't just leave for white Americans. The jobs leave for black Americans as well. But I think as far as there being some kind of concerted Civil Rights Movement, I don't think such an event will ever happen again in this country.

MM: Are you troubled by the current political climate with the tendency toward conservatism or neoconservatism?

GN: Well, this country has been in a conservative swing since the seventies. We've only had two Democratic presidents since the seventies—that is Jimmy Carter and Bill Clinton. And they are not what you might call liberal Democrats. You know, they were conservative Democrats. So what worries me is that the political scene seems to offer no viable choice to pick a leader with, because the Democrats have been running after the white male vote that they lost to the Republicans in the seventies and eighties, and they take for granted that they're going to get black support, Latino support, union support in what they're doing.

MM: So you're suggesting then that the Democratic Party has been moving toward currying favor with the white establishment while virtually ignoring the needs of black constituents?

GN: That's not what I'm suggesting; that's what I'm saying outright. That is definitely what I see happening, and it makes the country, it makes democracy less viable as a result. Because when people don't have a true choice, you know, that is why there is usually no excitement about elections. That is why we tend to have such a low voter turnout. But politicians are politicians. They're not always leaders. Because a world leader would look around and realize that there are other options. There are other votes available if the political leaders would decide to go after those as opposed to running after the status quo.

MM: How do you account for the optimism underlying your fictional works? When I take a look at your writing, from *The Women of Brewster Place* up until *The Men of Brewster Place,* it occurs to me that your characters are amazingly resilient. They tend to bounce back from tragedy and adversity, with the exception of the ones that commit suicide, like Laurel DuMont, or possibly Willa, or even Greasy in *The Men of Brewster Place.* Why do you think those characters are as resilient as they are?

GN: They are resilient because of my own belief in the power of the human spirit. My personal philosophy dictates that in spite of whatever situation you find yourself in, there can be a ray of hope. You can transcend any circumstance. Margaret Atwood, a wonderful writer, said that people without hope do not write books. So every time I sit down and I'm working on a book it is my little vote toward the continuation of the human spirit.

MM: Do you make a distinction between being spiritual and being religious?

GN: Yes, I do. For me, spirituality transcends religion. At one point in my life I was with the religious sect called the Jehovah's Witnesses because I believed in their philosophy that a theocracy was needed to solve our problems. The problems that society faced were just too rooted into the system. Therefore, one act or one law could not ameliorate what was wrong with this country or the world. They proposed a theocratic government that appealed to me at that time. In the sixties, I thought that I could believe in what they proposed. But I worked with them for seven years and saw no theocratic government coming. I was twenty-five years old at the time with a high school education and no marketable skills. So that is when I decided to go to college, which they didn't encourage in those years. Now they don't bother, but in those years they didn't encourage you to go to college. I decided I was going to go to college and gain a skill. I entered a nursing program and found myself spending more time with my English classes than with my nursing classes, so I transferred to Brooklyn College, where I majored in English literature. It was then that I began taking creative writing courses.

MM: Where do you position yourself with regard to orthodox Christianity? My students and I often engage in a debate about your authorial stance with regard to the Bible. Obviously, your familiarity with Scripture has played a major role in the fictional world you construct.

GN: I'm an outsider. After that experience with the Witnesses, I don't ascribe to any one religion. How can you? You know, there are so many different beliefs throughout the world and the majority of the world is not Christian. But I believe that spirituality is something that we can all share across religious lines. Spirituality comes from a place that is deeper than religion, as far as I am concerned. It comes from the same place that the inspiration for my writing emerges. I don't pooh-pooh people who are religious. It is better to be religious than nonreligious, I guess. So I don't discredit those efforts. It is just that I think that formalized religion is not for me. Too much dirt has been done in the name of religion throughout the centuries.

MM: Do you feel that the Bible has a message that is relevant for the younger generation, say, the hip-hop generation?

GN: I think the Bible has principles in that are relevant for any generation. There are viable principles within it that can be applied to any generation no matter what, you know. If we just boil it down to something as simple as the golden rule: "Do unto others as you would have them do unto you." If we just follow that premise, the world would go through a revolutionary change. But I think that the problem with the world today is not the Bible or the Koran or the Bhagavad Gita. I think that the problem is with the fact that people who ascribe to these religions don't really practice the principles of these religions. And so, I didn't, I never wanted to be boxed into a certain religion or precept but to allow my mind and my soul to go wherever it goes.

MM: I notice in your writing you tend to rely heavily upon biblical texts, especially in *Bailey's Café,* a novel in which many of the characters are named for biblical figures. You also tend to incorporate biblical numerology into your texts. And you are not shy about dealing with prophecy, particularly notions of an apocalyptic end to an oppressive social and political system.

GN: Well, I studied the Bible from the time I was thirteen until I was twenty-five. I mean, I was involved in really intense Bible study. So it's a book, a religious book that I know quite well. And as far as the women in Bailey's Café, I not only gave them names of women from the Bible, I retold the story of those biblical women because it always struck me as interesting that out of the sixty-six books of the Bible, only two of them have women's names.

MM: Ruth and Esther.

GN: Yes, Ruth and Esther. And if you look at the kind of women they were, these women were very subservient. And even as important a figure as the Virgin Mary is, she has very little to say, except I think in one of the gospels she says, "I am your handmaiden, do with me what you will" or something like that. Other than that, these women said nothing. So I wanted to listen to what Jezebel had to say, and what Eve had to say, and what Mary Magdalene had to say. And so I just revamped their stories into post–World War II personas.

MM: Do you view your writing as a calling?

GN: I don't know if it's a calling. That's kind of vaunted language. It is definitely a talent that I have. I know that I feel the most fulfilled when I'm engaged in writing in some way or another. But I don't think that some otherworldly being said, "Get her. That's the one." No, I don't think that happens, because you can have a God-given talent and you can waste it. And many people have done that. They have not utilized their God-given talents. So for me, it has been wonderful to take a talent that I did not give to myself, but to try to hone it and craft it into an occupation.

MM: Let's talk a little bit about your creation of character. Each of your characters is uniquely individual. Do you use a formula in naming them, or is it a situation where you feel as though the characters name themselves as they appear to you or manifest themselves to you?

GN: I think it's basically the latter, except sometimes I plot it out. I do. Like in *Linden Hills*, the fact that his name is Willie and her name is Willa is not coincidental, because they are two sides of the same coin and they are slowly moving toward each other. And their stories slowly, slowly, slowly become entwined. So that was done intentionally. Sometimes names will come to me first; sometimes the character will come to me first. It all depends.

MM: Could you comment on the relationship between art or writing and healing and therapy in your work, because you've said elsewhere, you've mentioned in interviews, that writing sort of saved your sanity. Do you feel as though your art has the ability to heal other people?

GN: Yes. I do. And not just the written art. You will notice there is a lot of art in my home. Well, if my house weren't all messed up from construction you would notice there is a lot of art in my home. There is also a lot of music in my home. I believe that the arts can heal. Because what they do, Maxine, is that they go to a place, this inexplicable place, that we cannot touch voluntarily. And from that—which I guess is the fountain-spring of your talent—and from that pours forth these works of art. And for people to heal, truly heal themselves, they have to go to that same kind of place. Pull up those same resources. Except the end result for them is survival of some disease or some physical situation. But music—they say music soothes the savage breast of the beast—I firmly believe that. I believe walking through a park in the springtime, looking at the beauty of the tulips, and the beauty of the trees budding out, is healing. Nature can be healing. So I don't say that every book that's ever written can heal you, because different books are written with different motives and goals in mind. But I do believe that art, as a general rule, can affect your spirituality. Sure.

MM: One of my favorite lines from *Bailey's Café* is the comment that Eve makes to Peaches's father when she says, "Leave your daughter here. I'll return her to you whole."

GN: I love that. I really love that. Yes. In other words, she was going to heal her by restoring Peaches's self-worth. Peaches had been fragmented because of her encounters with patriarchy. But Eve is the resident healer who accepts her unconditionally.

MM: Is it coincidental that only the women in your text have this gift of healing, whether we're talking about Mattie Michael, who heals Ciel after that traumatic event that Ciel goes through in *The Women of Brewster Place,* or we're talking about Eve in *Bailey's Café* or Miranda in *Mama Day?*

GN: Sure. Mama Day is a healer.

MM: The male characters don't seem to have the same therapeutic, healing quality associated with them.

GN: They don't. Yes, that's true. Until I got to *The Men of Brewster Place,* I hadn't really concentrated on the various aspects of the male personality. I was looking at women because traditionally, although they had been shamans, there are shamans in certain cultures and witch-doctors in some cultures, but the overwhelming weight of folk-healing has fallen on the shoulders of women, I think, at least the ones that have passed through Diaspora here to the United States, and these are the ones I know about.

MM: Why do you think that is? Do you think it has something to do with the perception that women have more of a connection with a spiritual realm than men do? Are you asserting that women possess certain intuitive powers?

GN: Well, I think maybe because it's just a leftover, could be just a leftover profession. The oppressed group tends to receive what the oppressors don't want. For example, with food, the slaves got the extremities of the hog while the master got the ham and the bacon and the slaves learned to make delicious dishes or soul food with the intestines of the animal, with the feet of the animal, with the ears of the animal, you know, with the less choicer parts. So I think probably for women, too, it was beneath many doctors in the medical profession to heal women, to deal with women, outside of childbirth. So other women took up that vacuum. Women stepped in and did what no one else wanted to do. But I don't think there is anything intrinsic in us that make us healers because I have seen how women can be destroyers too.

MM: That is very true. Let's talk about the ending of your first novel. Why is Ben's death necessary in *The Women of Brewster Place?* This is a question my students often pose. Why is his death necessary? Why is Willa's death needed in *Linden Hills?*

GN: Well, I'll talk about Ben first. I had to show that the community's isolation of Lorraine was a terminal situation. Here you have throughout the book women helping each other to overcome life-threatening situations, ego-threatening situations, sometimes very petty situations, but the women help each other. When it came to Lorraine, because of her sexual preference, that support system broke down, and the only voice of reason that was in that community about those two girls was the voice of Ben. He refused to go along with the gossipmongers like Sophie and he even befriended Lorraine. So there she is in that dark alley moving toward her own source of comfort that was given her, which was Ben, and she is raped, and I want that rape to reflect upon the whole community of women, for them to see that Lorraine wasn't raped because she was a lesbian; she was raped because she was a woman. And every woman in that block, I think I said from the ages of eighteen months to eighty years, dreamed of Lorraine, because her fate can be any woman's fate. So Ben's death just brought that lesson home more.

MM: And Willa in *Linden Hills:* Did you intend her death to be a suicide—and I know suicide is something that is a recurring emphasis in your work. Is Willa's death suicidal or self-sacrificial? Is she sacrificing herself in order to bring down this male dynasty?

GN: No. Not really. It's not a suicide. She had lost her mind in that basement, and what she was moving toward was what she understood—cleaning up, getting the house back in order, and it's in the irony of her doing this that that tree falls on her and Luther and the fire comes and burns them all up. But she's not trying to commit suicide; she's moving toward the only little bit of affirmation that she had left, and that was herself as a homemaker. So the irony is her death. But it's not that she had to die or she was fated to die or anything such as that.

MM: You talk often about Eva McKinney, and I believe you interviewed her at least on one occasion. How much of Eva McKinney is there in *Bailey's Café*'s Eve?

GN: Well, Eve's feeling toward her sexuality is very liberal. But Eva McKinney was really a prototype for Mama Day, not for Eve. Mama Day was the folk healer. She was the midwife. Mama Day is the quintessential woman. She was the nurse for that whole community the same way Eva McKinney functioned as a central maternal presence in Robinsonville, Mississippi.

MM: Is Eva McKinney still living?

GN: No. She was born Christmas Day 1900. No. She died years ago.

MM: What motivates Eve in *Bailey's Café* to take in all of those misfit women? How are we to see this very intriguing woman? What prompted you to create such a complex female character?

GN: Eve is a strange character. It appears that she is unsympathetic, but yet she reaches out her hand to help the most degenerate of her boarders. No. She is the mother of all women, but she is not a demonstrative mother. She sort of delves out harsh love. What do you call it?

MM: Tough love.

GN: Tough love. Exactly.

MM: That's it.

GN: Especially with Jessie. And I love that. I love those things between her and Jessie when they're in hell and Eve tries to break Jesse's addiction.

MM: And she does it, too.

GN: And she does it. And Jessie says that she felt during the whole ordeal that Eve didn't care if she lived or died. But Eve says, "I said to you when you were in thy own blood, live." Eve is definitely a healing, redemptive influence, not only for Jesse Bell but all of the women fortunate enough to find her brownstone.

MM: That's right. That's right. Of what importance is it that Eve gardens. I've noticed in your canon that a lot of the major female characters have a connection with the soil, whether it's Mattie Michael, who takes her plants with her to Brewster Place, or one of the Nedeed wives in *Linden Hills* who is banned from her garden. Eve, of course, has a garden that blooms year round in *Bailey's Café*, and Miranda has a garden, and Sapphira Wade has a garden as well in *Mama Day*. Of what importance is that connection with the land, or the soil, with those major female figures?

GN: Well, it's a cycle of fecundity. You know, you start out with a seed, and from that seed you get a plant. From that plant you get a flower, or a tomato, or a green pepper. You have created the same way that women during their pregnancies gestate and create as well. From a small seed all of this begins to happen. But the fact that Eve has a garden is because she is Eve. So that is part and parcel of being Eve. Except, rather than God having made this garden, she made it for herself. And she associates each of her female boarders with some type of flower.

MM: So it is her role to nurture those women and help them reach their potential, whatever that potential might be for that one individual?

GN: Exactly.

MM: To what do you attribute the emphasis in your work on houses or home or architectural space? I notice that in your work there tends to be a very heavy emphasis on space—tearing down walls, reconfiguring homes, escaping basements, and burning down houses. Not only that, but apartment complexes are razed, as is the case with Brewster Place, in order to make room for middle-income houses. Why is there such a preoccupation throughout your canon?

GN: I think it comes from my background. My parents were Mississippi sharecroppers. My mother and my father, for the first twenty years of their life, before they left and moved to New York, were cotton farmers. And I think it is part of my southern heritage that place has such an important part in my novels. Because as an African American with southern roots—and I have to specify that, because all African Americans do not have the same experience—but as far as I am concerned, as a result of my southern agricultural roots, people told my family to strive for a little bit of something for yourself. We were encouraged to have just a little bit of place, if you could. If you had a house that was yours, no one could throw you out and make you move. And that is the mentality of sharecroppers—people who were not allowed to own the land they worked. So I think my sense of place comes from that. It also comes from the fact that I invent these locales. I rarely write about a specific geographical location. The settings that I fashion, such as Brewster Place, Linden Hills, Willow Springs, and Bailey's Café, are all metaphysical situations that I write about. And so, because they are the character—the place is the character—I think I spend a lot of time trying to create it.

MM: Sure. Why were your grandmother's apartment buildings destroyed? What is the story behind that?

GN: There was a fire in 1967 and the apartments burned down, and so they just sold the land that those apartment buildings were situated on.

MM: Do you know what is there in that space now?

GN: Right now it's just empty. And so they have razed the whole block. The whole block is gone. So it's my guess they're going to put high-risers there.

MM: Do you go back to Robinsonville often?

GN: Not often. I went back when I was researching *Mama Day* in 1986, and that is when I met with Eva McKinney and did that interview. And Robinsonville was just about dying then.

MM: Really? What is its population?

GN: It was a sharecroppers' town. So I would say two or three hundred people.

MM: That is small.

GN: Yeah, it was very small. It was just a little place. It only came to be because of the migrant sharecroppers who settled there. And it was on this rich white man's land called Leatherman. So it was not even a major town. There was a post office and there were stores—a few little merchandising stores. I remember a juke joint, you know, but it never became a real city or anything of that nature. And in the 1940s, after many of the blacks, like my parents, left to go north or to the west, Robinsonville began to die. So when I went to see it in 1987 I wrote an essay about that for Nikki Giovanni's book about grandmothers. It was called *Telling Tales and Mississippi Sunsets*. So by that time Robinsonville was just about gone.

MM: Tell me about your experiences in Jacksonville, Florida. I know that you spent some time there when you were pioneering for the Jehovah's Witnesses.

GN: I was just about leaving the organization at that point.

MM: Do you have any specific or particular memories of Jacksonville?

GN: Nothing particular. I worked as a hotel switchboard operator at the Thunderbird Motel, and they used to have different acts come through the city, and so one time I saw Red Foxx in person. He was at the front desk. Other than that, I have no specific memories of the city.

MM: How would you describe the South's legacy for African American writers, both those who were born and stayed connected with the region like Zora Neal Hurston, or Richard Wright, and those who, like yourself, were not born there? You still have southern roots through the influence of your parents. How would you describe the legacy that the South has bequeathed to African American authors and do you think that legacy is the same for black authors as it is for white authors like William Faulkner, Eudora Welty, and others?

GN: Well, that's a good question. When black authors envisioned the South, it inevitably had to deal in some part or other with oppression, with the color line. When whites like William Faulkner or Eudora Welty envisioned the South, it was about its claustrophobia, for the most part. So you can look at Richard Wright and Eudora Welty, for example, who were both from Jackson, and look at the difference between *Native Son* and *The Optimist's Daughter.* So I think your work comes from your world view. Your world view comes from the world that you were given to deal with, and we have been, for a very, very long time, two separate nations.

MM: At what point in your career did you become interested in telling the male story?

GN: Well, I have always had men in my books, and I disagreed with the critics who said that the men were two-dimensional because even when they had small parts I tried to make them as multidimensional as I could. I tried very hard to give them a measure of depth and complexity.

MM: Abshu has a moderate level of complexity in your latest novel. In fact, in *The Men of Brewster Place,* all the men are well rounded. Ben is complex in your first book.

GN: Yes, in the first book, Ben is well rounded. I had no axe to grind as far as male character is concerned. Keep in mind that my whole purpose was to celebrate the black female experience. This means that men had walk-on parts. For example, in *Mama Day,* one-third of that book is carried by a male voice—George Andrews. So I've never disregarded men in my work, but central to my work is some aspect of the black female experience. And I don't apologize for that.

MM: Was there trepidation on your part in creating male character, or were you as confident in creation of male character as you were in your creation of female characters such as Eve?

GN: Early on, when I was contemplating *Linden Hills* and I knew that half of the book would have to be carried by two twenty-year-old black males, I was a little intimidated. And I said to myself, well, what do I know about being a black male? And the answer was, very little. So what I did was write letters to Willie Mason and I explained to him what I wanted to do, and that I had some hesitation because I didn't want to do it wrong. Of course, I could write convincingly about the lives of black men. But I wanted to write about them with some depth and some sensitivity. So writing those letters to that fictive character helped me to open up and to see that men and women have a lot in common. It's just that we have made whole industries out of our differences, but in reality most people in the world have a lot in common. Who doesn't want a sane life, with good health, with enough to eat, with a warm place to sleep, with friends and family? Who doesn't want that all over the whole universe? Men want that as well as women. It's just that because of our socialization those desires get manifested differently.

MM: Talk about *The Men of Brewster Place*. There's a character in there by the name of Brother Jerome, the young man that plays the blues. Of all the male characters in that text, the male characters who have stories in that text, he's the one that does not appear in the first novel, *The Women of Brewster Place*.

GN: Yes, he is the background music as he plays the blues. He's playing the blues for the other male characters who come up, because each of their stories has some aspect of the blues in it. You know, like losing a woman, losing a mother, having a no-good woman, trying to find yourself, being unemployed, that kind of thing.

MM: So he brings a measure of unity to novel.

GN: He's supposed to be the background riff for all of these stories. Because I think when you get to Abshu's story and they're going to condemn the buildings and Abshu says, "Someone should stop that boy from playing," the music was just playing in his head.

MM: What's the inspiration behind "Miss Maple's Blues" in *Bailey's Café?* And that story is the longest story in the novel. What's the story behind "Miss Maple's Blues"? You said in another interview that you consider Miss Maple to be the manliest man that you know.

GN: A man has to be very sure of his sexuality to go around dressing in drag everyday. He has to be sure of what defines him as a man.

MM: I taught *Bailey's Café* a couple of years ago, and as a final project my students had to deliver a fifteen- to twenty-minute oral presentation based on their research essay. One of the male students who wrote a paper on *Bailey's Café* came to class dressed as he thought Miss Maple would. He came to class in a house dress.

GN: Did he really? Oh my goodness! That's amusing. Was his paper any good?

MM: It was good. It was a good paper. Yes it was. So I was just wondering what the impetus was behind the creation of a Miss Maple. What truths are you presenting concerning constructions of masculinity?

GN: Miss Maple was to be a bookend for Bailey. Bailey did all the things that would help to define him as a man, right? He grew up. He fell in love with a woman. He went to war, right? He did those things that they tell you are manly things. Miss Maple, on the other hand, did not chase women. He was a conscientious objector in the war, right? And he ultimately got into this bizarre situation where he was wearing women's clothes because they were comfortable for him. So what I was trying to look at were two different parts of masculinity. Miss Maple is just as masculine as Bailey was, although he made different choices in life.

MM: So masculinity is not monolithic. It is socially constructed.

GN: Masculinity is not monolithic, and also he defined for himself what it means to be a man. See, the world has said if you're a male you have to put on certain clothes, you have to adopt a certain posture. Well, Miss Maple said, in a sense, I am a man, and I don't have to wear those clothes. I don't have to adopt those postures.

And I'm still as much of a man as anyone is because he didn't have to question his sexuality.

MM: Of what importance is it that the closing scene in *The Men of Brewster Place* takes place in a barbershop?

GN: Because that's where men gather. That is their equivalent of a female coffee klatch. They gather there, chew over the events of the world, and they chew over their relationships. They do all of this in a barbershop. So I thought, what better place to have all of the men come together except in that barbershop?

MM: Have you seen the movie *Barbershop?*

GN: I have not. I heard there was controversy over it because they denounced Martin Luther King.

MM: And there was a disparagement of Rosa Parks as well.

GN: Oh really? No, I have not seen it.

MM: How are we to interpret the Shakespeare connection in "Miss Maple's Blues"? There is a scene where Stanley's father is attempting to ship volumes of Shakespeare's works and the Gatlins try to confiscate those books and they urinate on the books. There's a line that says, "The stench of *The Tempest* filled the storeroom." Critics have talked a lot about the Shakespeare connection in your writing. I'm wondering how that connection figures into "Miss Maple's Blues."

GN: Well, it was part of it. I've always, like you said, used Shakespeare in some way, shape, or form in my work up until *The Men of Brewster Place.* Yes, I did. I used it there too because he taught the children to curse like Shakespearean characters. I was bitten by the bug very early in my life concerning William Shakespeare. I used to love to read *Romeo and Juliet,* and we had a small house in Queens, and it was a two-story house, and I would be at the bottom of the steps, and I would be Romeo. Then I'd run up to the top of the steps and I'd pretend to be Juliet. This is how I used to amuse myself. Now, Miss Maple and Shakespeare were just connected that way. His father wanted him to think beyond the box, for the most part. And if you're looking for an artist to do that, that was definitely

William Shakespeare. He did not allow his imagination to stay just with Elizabethan English society. He took us to Rome, right? He took us to Denmark. He took us to the Caribbean in *The Tempest,* as a matter of fact. So he was a man who really introduced brave new worlds, and I think that's why Stanley's father, Miss Maple's father, wanted to give him those volumes.

MM: One critic has labeled your representation of gay/lesbian relations as being tragic or bleak. How do you respond to that?

GN: They are no more tragic or bleak than my other relationships. You know, I have not ever been credited with being a ha-ha-ha writer. I take on some heavy topics, and my world vision sometimes is quite dark. And I'm aware of that. But I don't single out gay people to be any more tragic than straight people.

MM: How do you want to be remembered as a novelist?

GN: I want to be remembered as a good, good, good storyteller. I think the more you keep it simple, the greater your reach is going to be as far as who you affect. You have a story. I have a story. Everyone has a story. And it is important that I tell that story as succinctly and as honestly as I can.

MM: Thank you. I so appreciate your taking time to share your insights with me and for welcoming me into your home.

GN: Yes. My pleasure.

* * *

As a follow-up to the May 3 interview, and in light of the historic election of Barack Obama as the nation's first African American president, I contacted Naylor by phone on February 3, 2009, and asked a series of questions.

MM: What do you think the likely impact of the Obama presidency will be as far as race relations are concerned?

GN: Little, if any. He came out of a Senate in the twenty-first century where he was only the third African American senator since Reconstruction. Black candidates have a problem garnering broad support outside of local elections for mayors or congressional representatives. The Obama victory was a "perfect storm" of having a candidate who was psychologically comfortable for the white male voter because he loved their mothers and he didn't want to marry their daughters, thus removing the eight-hundred-pound gorilla of their fear of black male sexuality along with any guilt for this country's treatment of the descendants of African American slaves—his father wasn't even a *West* African—combined with an increasingly Latino immigrant nation who identified with yet another mulatto and his family's immigrant story combined with the desperation of youths for change in an overwhelmingly failing economy that guaranteed them little security in their future combined with a highly effective grass-roots high-tech campaign. Unique. Singular. And I predict that, like our first Catholic president, it's a feat that won't be repeated for generations to come. There's no groundswell in the African American political community under this "perfect storm": Our politicians remain, for the most part, imitative, mediocre and/or opportunistic.

MM: Do you see the election as being an event that will move the country forward in the quest for race, class, and gender equality?

GN: Not the election itself but, perhaps, the ideals of the president himself. This country doesn't have a history of being aggressive in any quest for race, class, or gender equality. Our government dropped the ball for true racial equality during Reconstruction when meaningful reparations could have been made to African Americans instead of their being abandoned in the Tilden/Hayes election in exchange for southern support of the Hayes candidacy, which brought in the infamous black codes. And the Equal Rights Amendment lost its bid for a majority of state ratification in the seventies. And as far as class, we need only look at the constitution to see the mindset of the founding fathers. Only land-owning white male citizens had the right to vote, and then only for president through the Electoral College—hardly a representative democracy. However, President Obama seems committed to greater parity than has evolved in this government from the constitution.

MM: Might the recent election inspire a new wave of community activism? After all, Barack Obama was extremely successful at strategizing his campaign for change in such a way as to garner a great deal of support at the grass-roots level. I tend to compare the level of enthusiasm surrounding his candidacy to the fervor associated with the Civil Rights Movement.

GN: I hope so. It's only from the grass roots that any true change has come. And if not his personal efforts in the past, which are admirable, perhaps, his victory as a grass-roots candidate will serve as evidence that such tactics can be highly successful in the face of overwhelming odds and resistance.

MM: What do you think his priorities should be during his term in office?

GN: The economy. The economy. The economy. This will benefit all communities, harkening back to Jesse Jackson's metaphor of all boats rising as the waters rise. And hopefully, he will act in order to place stricter regulations on the mortgage and banking institutions.

MM: One last thing. Those of us who are intrigued by your work and especially *Mama Day* would like to know when you expect to finalize "Sapphira," the novel that is to fictionalize the relationship between the Willow Springs foremother and Bascombe Wade.

GN: It is going to be a while before "Sapphira" is complete. I am about one-third of the way finished with the novel.

Notes

Introduction

1. Angels Carabi, "An Interview with Gloria Naylor," *Conversations with Gloria Naylor*, ed. Maxine Lavon Montgomery (Jackson: UP of Mississippi, 2004), 114, 118–19.

2. See the personal interview, "Opening Up the Place Called Home: A Conversation with Gloria Naylor," May 3, 2007, included in the appendix. Subsequent references to this interview are included parenthetically in the text; Gloria Naylor, "Finding Our Voice," *Essence* 26 (May 1995): 193; Donna Perry, "Gloria Naylor," *Conversations with Gloria Naylor*, ed. Maxine Lavon Montgomery (Jackson: UP of Mississippi, 2004), 76–104; Carabi 77 and 111; Willard Pate, "Do You Think of Yourself as a Woman Writer?" *Furman Studies* 34 (December 1988): 2–13; and untitled interview in Rebecca Carroll, ed., *I Know What the Red Clay Looks Like: The Voice and Vision of Black Women Writers* (New York: Crown, 1994), 16.

3. Abdul R. JanMohamed, "Worldliness—Without World, Homelessness as Home: Toward a Definition of the Specular Border Intellectual," *Edward Said: A Critical Reader*, ed. Michael Sprinkler (Cambridge: Blackwell, 1992).

4. Bracha Ettinger, *The Matrixial Borderspace* (Minneapolis: U of Minnesota P, 2006), 41–89.

5. William Goldstein, "A Talk with Gloria Naylor," *Conversations with Gloria Naylor*, ed. Maxine Lavon Montgomery (Jackson: UP of Mississippi, 2004), 6.

6. Victor Turner, *Dramas, Fields, and Metaphors: Symbolic Action in Human Society* (Ithaca: Cornell UP, 1974), 13–14.

Chapter 1

1. Goldstein; Kay Bonetti, "An Interview with Gloria Naylor," *Conversations with Gloria Naylor*, ed. Maxine Lavon Montgomery (Jackson: UP of Mississippi, 2004); and Carabi 5, 54, 119.

2. Gloria Naylor, "An Interview," online interview, Barnes and Noble, May 12, 1998 <http://www.aalb.com/authors/glorianaylorchattext.htm>.

3. Gloria Naylor, *The Women of Brewster Place* (New York: Viking, 1982), 25. Subsequent references to this work are included parenthetically in the text.

4. Gloria Naylor and Toni Morrison, "A Conversation," *Conversations with Gloria Naylor,* ed. Maxine Lavon Montgomery (Jackson: UP of Mississippi, 2004), 10–12.

5. Carabi 115.

6. See Michael Awkward, "Authorial Dreams of Wholeness: (Dis) Unity, (Literary) Parentage, and *The Women of Brewster Place,*" *Gloria Naylor: Critical Perspectives Past and Present,* ed. Henry L. Gates Jr. and K. A. Appiah (New York: Amistad, 1993), 37–70.

7. Jenny Brantley, "Women's Screams and Women's Laughter: Connections and Creations in Gloria Naylor's Novels," *Gloria Naylor's Early Novels,* ed. Margot Anne Kelley (Gainesville: UP of Florida, 1999), 21–38.

8. Jill L. Matus, "Dream, Deferral, and Closure in *The Women of Brewster Place,*" *Gloria Naylor: Critical Perspectives Past and Present,* ed. Henry L. Gates Jr. and K. A. Appiah (New York: Amistad, 1993), 136.

9. Perry 81–82.

10. Joanne Gabbin, "A Laying on of Hands: Black Women Writers Exploring the Roots of Their Folk and Cultural Tradition," *Wild Women in the Whirlwind: Afra-American Culture and the Contemporary Literary Renaissance,* ed. Joanne Braxton and Andree Nicola McLaughlin (New Brunswick: Rutgers UP, 1990), 246–62.

11. Brantley 21–38.

Chapter 2

1. Gloria Naylor, *Linden Hills* (New York: Ticknor and Fields, 1985), 17. Subsequent references to this work are included parenthetically in the text.

2. Henry Louis Gates Jr., "Significant Others," *Contemporary Literature* 29 (1988): 606–23.

3. Naomi Epel, "Gloria Naylor," *Writers Dreaming* (New York: Carol Southern, 1993), 163.

4. Perry 91.

5. Bonetti 47.

6. Kimberly Costino, "Weapons Against Women: Compulsory Heterosexuality and Capitalism in *Linden Hills*," *Gloria Naylor's Early Novels,* ed. Margot Anne Kelley (Gainesville: UP of Florida, 1999), 39–54.

7. Perry 90.

8. Mickey Pearlman and Katherine Henderson, "Gloria Naylor," *Conversations with Gloria Naylor,* ed. Maxine Lavon Montgomery (Jackson: UP of Mississippi, 2004), 71.

9. Naylor and Morrison 31–32; and Perry 90.

10. See Margaret Homans, "The Woman in the Cave," *Gloria Naylor: Critical Perspectives Past and Present,* ed. Henry L. Gates Jr. and K. A. Appiah (New York: Amistad, 1993), 152–81; and Teresa Goddu, "Reconstructing History in *Linden Hills*," *Gloria Naylor: Critical Perspectives Past and Present,* ed. Henry L. Gates Jr. and K. A. Appiah (New York: Amistad, 1993), 215–30.

Chapter 3

1. Dorothy Perry Thompson, "Africana Womanist Revision in Gloria Naylor's *Mama Day*," *Gloria Naylor's Early Novels,* ed. Margot Anne Kelley (Gainesville: UP of Florida, 1999), 90.

2. Susan Meisenhelder, "False Gods and Black Goddesses in Naylor's *Mama Day* and Hurston's *Their Eyes Were Watching God*," *Callaloo* 23.4 (2000): 1440–48.

3. Gloria Naylor, *Mama Day* (New York: Random, 1989), 3. Subsequent references to this work are included parenthetically in the text.

4. See Meisenhelder, "The Whole Picture in Gloria Naylor's *Mama Day*," *The Critical Response to Gloria Naylor,* ed. Sharon Felton and Michelle Loris (Westport: Greenwood, 1977), 113–28; Lindsey Tucker, "Recovering the Conjure Woman: Texts and Contexts in Gloria Naylor's

Mama Day," *African-American Review* 28 (Summer 1994): 173–88; Teresa N. Washington, *Our Mothers, Our Powers, Our Texts: Manifestations of Aje in Africana Literature* (Bloomington: Indiana UP, 2008); and Daphne Lamothe, "Gloria Naylor's *Mama Day:* Bridging Roots and Routes," *African-American Review* 39.1, 2 (2005): 155–69.

5. Virginia Fowler, *Gloria Naylor: In Search of Sanctuary* (New York: Twayne, 1996), 148.

6. Julie B. Farwell, "Goophering Around: Authority and the Trick of Storytelling in Charles W. Chesnutt's *The Conjure Woman,"* *Tricksterism in Turn-of-the-Century American Literature,* ed. Elizabeth Ammons and Annette White-Parks (Hanover: UP of New England, 1994), 80–94.

7. Tucker 173–88.

8. Sherley Anne Williams, *Dessa Rose* (New York: Berkley, 1986), 10.

9. Lamothe 156.

10. Suzette Spencer, "Reexamining the Relationship Between Thomas Jefferson and Sally Hemmings," lecture, February 9, 2006, Florida State University, Tallahassee.

11. See Karla Lewis Gottlieb, *A History of Queen Nanny: Leader of the Winward Jamaican Maroons* (Trenton: Africa World, 2000); and Mark Smith, *Stono: Documenting and Interpreting a Southern Slave Revolt* (Columbia: U of South Carolina P, 2005).

12. Tucker 112.

13. Helene Christol, "Reconstructing American History: Land and Genealogy in Gloria Naylor's *Mama Day,"* *The Critical Response to Gloria Naylor,* ed. Sharon Felton and Michelle Loris (Westport: Greenwood, 1997), 164.

14. Meisenhelder, "Whole Picture" 116.

15. Meisenhelder, "Whole Picture" 125.

16. Lamothe 168.

17. Perry 93.

18. Untitled interview in Carroll 160–61.

Chapter 4

1. Gloria Naylor, *Bailey's Café* (New York: Harcourt, Brace, Jovanovich, 1992). Subsequent references to this work are included parenthetically in the text.

2. D. C. Denison, "Gloria Naylor," *Boston Globe Magazine* December 1994: 7, and Fowler 146.

3. Thompson 103.

4. Thompson 102.

5. Patti Doten, "Naylor in Her Glory," *Boston Globe Magazine*, October 1992: 81.

6. See Deirdre Good, "What Does It Mean to Call Mary Mariam?" *A Feminist Companion to Mariology*, ed. Amy-Jill Levine (New York: Continnuum, 2005), 99–106.

7. Thompson 107.

Conclusion

1. Carabi 111, 120; Naylor, "Finding Our Voice" 193.

2. Mae Gwendolyn Henderson, *Borders, Boundaries, and Frames: Essays in Cultural Criticism and Cultural Studies* (New York: Routledge, 1995); and Carol Boyce Davies, *Black Women, Writing and Identity* (New York: Routledge, 1994).

Bibliography

Aptheker, Herbert. "Resistance and Afro-American History: Some Notes on Contemporary Historiography and Suggestions for Further Research." *In Resistance: Studies in African, Caribbean, and Afro-American History.* Ed. Gary Y. Okihiro. Amherst: U of Massachusetts P, 1986. 10–20.

Awkward, Michael. "Authorial Dreams of Wholeness: (Dis)Unity, (Literary) Parentage, and *The Women of Brewster Place.*" *Gloria Naylor: Critical Perspectives Past and Present.* Ed. Henry L. Gates Jr. and K. A. Appiah. New York: Amistad, 1993. 37–70.

Bachelard, Gaston. *The Poetics of Space.* New York: Orion, 1964.

Baker, Houston A. *Blues, Ideology, and Afro-American Literature: A Vernacular Theory.* Chicago: U of Chicago P, 1984.

Begg, Ean. *The Cult of the Black Virgin.* New York: Penguin, 1985.

Bell, Bernard W. *The Contemporary African-American Novel: Its Folk Roots and Modern Literary Branches.* Amherst: U of Massachusetts P, 2004.

Bhabha, Homi. *The Location of Culture.* New York: Routledge, 2004.

Bonetti, Kay. "An Interview with Gloria Naylor." *Conversations with Gloria Naylor.* Ed. Maxine Lavon Montgomery. Jackson: UP of Mississippi, 2004. 39–64.

Brantley, Jenny. "Women's Screams and Women's Laughter: Connections and Creations in Gloria Naylor's Novels." *Gloria Naylor's Early Novels.* Ed. Margot Anne Kelley. Gainesville: UP of Florida, 1999. 21–38.

Carabi, Angels. "An Interview with Gloria Naylor." *Conversations with Gloria Naylor.* Ed. Maxine Lavon Montgomery. Jackson: UP of Mississippi, 2004. 111–22.

Carroll, Rebecca, ed. *I Know What the Red Clay Looks Like: The Voices and Vision of Black Women Writers.* New York: Crown, 1994.

Christol, Helene. "Reconstructing American History: Land and Genealogy in Gloria Naylor's *Mama Day.*" *The Critical Response to Gloria Naylor.* Ed. Sharon Felton and Michelle Loris. Westport: Greenwood, 1997. 159–65.

Costino, Kimberly. "Weapons Against Women: Compulsory Hetero-sexuality and Capitalism in *Linden Hills.*" *Gloria Naylor's Early Novels.* Ed. Margot Anne Kelley. Gainesville: UP of Florida, 1999. 39–54.

Davies, Carol Boyce. *Migrations of the Subject: Black Women, Writing, and Identity.* New York: Routledge, 1994.

Davis, Angela. *Blues Legacies and Black Feminism: Gertrude "Ma" Rainey, Bessie Smith, and Billie Holiday.* New York: Random, 1998.

——. *Women, Race, and Class.* New York: Random, 1981.

Denison, D. C. "Gloria Naylor." *Boston Globe Magazine,* December 1994: 7.

Doten, Patti. "Naylor in Her Glory." *Boston Globe Magazine,* October 1992.

Du Bois, W. E. B. *The Souls of Black Folk.* New York: New American Library, 1969.

Epel, Naomi. "Gloria Naylor." *Writers Dreaming.* New York: Carol Southern, 1993.

Ettinger, Bracha. *The Matrixial Borderspace.* Minneapolis: U of Minnesota P, 2006.

Fanon, Frantz. *Black Skin, White Masks.* New York: Grove, 1967.

Farwell, Julie. "Authority and the Trick of Storytelling in Charles Waddell Chesnutt's *The Conjure Woman.*" *Tricksterism in Turn-of-the-Century American Literature.* Ed. Elizabeth Ammons and Annette White-Parks. Hanover: UP of New England, 1994. 80–94.

Fowler, Virginia. *Gloria Naylor: In Search of Sanctuary.* New York: Twayne, 1996.

Fox-Genovese, Elizabeth. "Strategies and Forms of Resistance: Focus on Slave Women in the United States. In *Resistance.* Ed. Gary Y. Okihiro. Amherst: U of Massachusetts P, 1986. 143–65.

Gabbin, Joanne. "A Laying on of Hands: Black Women Writers Exploring the Roots of Their Folk and Cultural Traditions." *Wild Women in the Whirlwind: Afra-American Culture and the Contemporary Literary Renaissance.* Ed. Joanne Braxton and Andree Nicola McLaughlin. New Brunswick: Rutgers UP, 1990.

Gates, Henry Louis, Jr. *The Signifying Monkey: A Theory of African-American Literary Criticism.* New York: Oxford UP, 1988.

Giddens, Paula. *When and Where I Enter: The Impact of Black Women on Race and Sex in America.* New York: Bantam, 1984.

Gilbert, Sandra, and Susan Gubar. *The Madwoman in the Attic: The Woman Writer and the Nineteenth Century Literary Imagination.* New Haven: Yale UP, 1979.

Gilroy, Paul. *The Black Atlantic: Modernity and Double Consciousness.* Cambridge: Harvard UP, 1992.

Goddu, Teresa. "Reconstructing History in *Linden Hills.*" *Gloria Naylor: Critical Perspectives Past and Present.* Ed. Henry L. Gates Jr. and K. A. Appiah. New York: Amistad, 1993. 215–30.

Goldstein, William. "A Talk with Gloria Naylor." *Conversations with Gloria Naylor.* Ed. Maxine Lavon Montgomery. Jackson: UP of Mississippi, 2004. 3–6.

Good, Deirdre. "What Does It Mean to Call Mary Mariam?" *A Feminist Companion to Mariology.* Ed. Amy-Jill Levine. New York: Continuum, 2005.

Gottlieb, Karla. *The Mother of Us All: A History of Queen Nanny, Leader of the Windward Jamaican Maroons.* Trenton: African World P, 2000.

Griffin, Farah Jasmine. *"Who Set You Flowin'?" The African-American Migration Narrative.* New York: Oxford UP, 1995.

Henderson, Mae Gwendolyn. *Borders, Boundaries, and Frames: Essays in Cultural Criticism and Cultural Studies.* New York: Routledge, 1995.

Hill-Collins, Patricia. *Black Feminist Thought: Knowledge, Consciousness, and the Politics of Empowerment.* New York: Routledge, 1991.

Homans, Margaret. "The Woman in the Cave." *Gloria Naylor: Critical Perspectives Past and Present.* Ed. Henry L. Gates Jr. and K. A. Appiah. New York: Amistad, 1993. 152–81.

hooks, bell. *Yearning: Race, Gender, and Cultural Politics.* Boston: South End, 1990.

Hurston, Zora Neale. *Mules and Men.* Bloomington: Indiana UP, 1935.

JanMohamed, Abdul. "Worldliness—Without World, Homelessness as Home: Toward a Definition of the Specular Border Intellectual." *Edward Said: A Critical Reader.* Ed. Michael Sprinkler. Cambridge: Blackwell, 1992.

Jones, Jacqueline. *Labor of Love, Labor of Sorrow: Black Women, Work, and the Family, from Slavery to the Present.* New York: Random House, 1985.

Jones-Jackson, Patricia. *When Roots Die: Endangered Traditions from the Sea Islands.* Athens: U of Georgia P, 1987.

Kelley, Margot Anne, ed. *Gloria Naylor's Early Novels*. Gainesville: UP of Florida, 1999.

Lamothe, Daphne. "Gloria Naylor's *Mama Day:* Bridging Roots and Routes." *African-American Review* 39.1, 2 (2005): 155–69.

Matus, Jill L. "Dream, Deferral, and Closure in *The Women of Brewster Place*." *Gloria Naylor: Critical Perspectives Past and Present*. Ed. Henry L. Gates Jr. and K. A. Appiah. New York: Amistad. 126–39.

Meisenhelder, Susan. "False Gods and Black Goddesses in Naylor's *Mama Day* and Hurston's *Their Eyes Were Watching God*." *Callaloo* 23.4 (2000): 1440–48.

——. "The Whole Picture in Gloria Naylor's *Mama Day*." *The Critical Response to Gloria Naylor*. Ed. Sharon Felton and Michelle Loris. Westport: Greenwood, 1977. 113–28.

Mellon, Joelle. *The Virgin Mary in the Perceptions of Women: Mother, Protector and Queen Since the Middle Ages*. Jefferson: McFarland, 2008.

Morrison, Toni. "Home." *The House that Race Built*. Ed. Wahneema Lubiano. New York: Random, 1998. 3–12.

Naylor, Gloria. *Bailey's Café*. New York: Harcourt, 1992.

——. "Finding Our Voice." *Essence* 26 (May 1995): 193.

——. "Hers." *New York Times* 20 (February 1986): C2.

——. "An Interview." Online interview. Barnes and Noble. May 12, 1998. <http://www.aalb.com/authors/glorianaylorchattext.htm>.

——. *Linden Hills*. New York: Ticknor and Fields, 1985.

——. *Mama Day*. New York: Random, 1988.

——. "Telling Tales and Mississippi Sunsets." *Grand Mothers: Poems, Reminiscences, and Stories About Keepers of Our Traditions*. Ed. Nikki Giovanni. New York: Henry Holt, 1994. 59–62.

——. Untitled interview. *I Know What the Red Clay Looks Like: The Voice and Vision of Black Women Writers*. Ed. Rebecca Carroll. New York: Crown Trade Paperbacks, 1994.

——. *The Women of Brewster Place*. New York: Penguin, 1982.

Naylor, Gloria, and Toni Morrison. "A Conversation." *Conversations with Gloria Naylor*. Ed. Maxine Lavon Montgomery. Jackson: UP of Mississippi, 2004. 10–38.

Okonkwo, Christopher N. "Suicide or Self Sacrifice: Exhuming Willa's Body in Gloria Naylor's *Linden Hills*." *African-American Review* 35.1 (Spring 2001): 117–31.

Pate, Willard. "Do You Think of Yourself as a Woman Writer?" *Furman Studies* 34 (December 1988): 2–13.

Pearlman, Mickey, and Katherine Usher Henderson. "Gloria Naylor." *Conversations with Gloria Naylor.* Ed. Maxine Lavon Montgomery. Jackson: UP of Mississippi, 2004. 70–75.

Perry, Donna. "Gloria Naylor." *Conversations with Gloria Naylor.* Ed. Maxine Lavon Montgomery. Jackson: UP of Mississippi, 2004. 76–104.

Prince, Valerie Sweeney. *Burnin' Down the House: Home in African-American Literature.* New York: Columbia UP, 2005.

Rabuzzi, Kathryn. *The Sacred and the Feminine: Toward a Theology of Housework.* New York: Seabury P, 1982.

Rowell, Charles H. "An Interview with Gloria Naylor." *Conversations with Gloria Naylor.* Ed. Maxine Lavon Montgomery. Jackson: UP of Mississippi, 2004. 151–67.

Sertima, Ivan Van. *Black Women in Antiquity.* New Brunswick: Transaction, 1985.

Smith, Barbara. *Homegirls.* New York: Kitchen Table P, 1983. xxi–lvi.

Smith, Mark. *Stono: Documenting and Interpreting a Southern Slave Revolt.* Columbia: U of South Carolina P, 2005.

Smitherman, Geneva. *Black Talk: Words and Phrases from the Hood to the Amen Corner.* New York: Houghton Mifflin, 2000.

———. *Word from the Mother: Language and African-Americans.* New York: Routledge, 2006.

Spencer, Suzette. "Reexamining the Relationship Between Thomas Jefferson and Sally Hemmings." Lecture. Florida State Univ., Tallahassee. February 9, 2006.

Spillers, Hortense. "Mama's Baby, Papa's Maybe: An American Grammar Book." *Within the Circle.* Ed. Angelyn Mitchell. Durham: Duke UP. 454–81.

Tucker, Lindsey. "Recovering the Conjure Woman: Texts and Contexts in Gloria Naylor's *Mama Day*." *African-American Review* 28 (Summer 1994): 173–88.

Turner, Victor. *Dramas, Fields, and Metaphors: Symbolic Action in Human Society.* Ithaca: Cornell UP, 1974.

Washington, Teresa N. *Our Mothers, Our Powers, Our Texts: Manifestations of Aje in Africana Literature.* Bloomington: Indiana UP, 2005.

Whitt, Margaret Early. *Understanding Gloria Naylor.* Columbia: U of South Carolina P, 1999.

Williams, Sherley Anne. *Dessa Rose.* New York: Berkley, 1986.

Willis, Susan. *Specifying: Black Women Writing the American Experience.* Madison: U of Wisconsin P, 1987.

Index

The Fiction of Gloria Naylor was designed and typeset on a Macintosh computer system using InDesign software. The body text is set in 11/15 Kepler and display type is set in Kepler. This book was designed and typeset by Chad Pelton, and manufactured by Thomson-Shore, Inc.